Shamans

New and future titles in the series include:

Alien Abductions
Angels
Atlantis
The Bermuda Triangle
The Curse of King Tut
The Devil
The Disappearance of Amelia Earhart
Dragons
Dreams
ESP
The Extinction of the Dinosaurs
Extraterrestrial Life
Fairies
Fortune-Telling
Ghosts
Haunted Houses
The Kennedy Assassination
King Arthur
The Loch Ness Monster
Mysterious Places
Poltergeists
Possessions and Exorcisms
Pyramids
Stonehenge
UFOs
Unicorns
Vampires
Witches

The Mystery Library

Shamans

Stuart A. Kallen

LUCENT BOOKS

An imprint of Thomson Gale, a part of The Thomson Corporation

Detroit • New York • San Francisco • San Diego • New Haven, Conn. • Waterville, Maine • London • Munich

LIBRARY OF CONGRESS CATALOGING-IN-PUBLICATION DATA

Kallen, Stuart A., 1955–
  Shamans / by Stuart A. Kallen.
    p. cm. — (The mystery library)
  Includes bibliographical references and index.
  ISBN 1-59018-628-1
  1. Shamanism. I. Title. II. Series: Mystery Library (Lucent Books).
  BL2370. S5K33 2004
  201'.44—dc22

                                        2004012665

Contents

Foreword   6

Introduction   8
     The Mystery of Shamanism

Chapter One   12
     An Enduring Tradition

Chapter Two   29
     Communicating with the Spirits

Chapter Three   47
     Healers

Chapter Four   62
     Evil Shamans

Chapter Five   78
     Shamans in the New Age

Notes   97
For Further Reading   101
Works Consulted   102
Index   106
Picture Credits   111
About the Author   112

Foreword

In Shakespeare's immortal play Hamlet, the young Danish aristocrat Horatio has clearly been astonished and disconcerted by his encounter with a ghostlike apparition on the castle battlements. "There are more things in heaven and earth," his friend Hamlet assures him, "than are dreamt of in your philosophy."

Many people today would readily agree with Hamlet, that the world and the vast universe surrounding it are teeming with wonders and oddities that remain largely outside the realm of present human knowledge or understanding. How did the universe begin? What caused the dinosaurs to become extinct? Was the lost continent of Atlantis a real place or merely legendary? Does a monstrous creature lurk beneath the surface of Scotland's Loch Ness? These are only a few of the intriguing questions that remain unanswered, despite the many great strides made by science in recent centuries.

Lucent Books' Mystery Library series is dedicated to exploring these and other perplexing, sometimes bizarre, and often disturbing or frightening wonders. Each volume in the series presents the best-known tales, incidents, and evidence surrounding the topic in question. Also included are the opinions and theories of scientists and other experts who have attempted to unravel and solve the ongoing mystery. And supplementing this information is a fulsome list of sources for further reading, providing the reader with the means to pursue the topic further.

The Mystery Library will satisfy every young reader's fascination for the unexplained. As one of history's greatest scientists, physicist Albert Einstein, put it:

The most beautiful thing we can experience is the mysterious. It is the source of all true art and science. He to whom this emotion is a stranger, who can no longer wonder and stand rapt in awe, is as good as dead: his eyes are closed.

The Mystery of Shamanism

In the seventeenth century, European explorers first traveled to the frozen forests of Siberia. In this isolated part of northeastern Russia, deep snow covers the ground up to nine months out of the year, and temperatures dip to 40 degrees Fahrenheit below zero in the winter. While hunting for reindeer and other valuable game, these European traders encountered indigenous people of the Tungus tribe who claimed to live in harmony with nature while communicating with spirits of plants and animals. In the Tungus language, these men and women were called *samans* or *shamans*.

Tungus shamans were mainly healers—the doctors of their society. But they also said that they could predict where game could be found, see into the future, and control the weather. A few of them practiced black magic and claimed they could cause their enemies to suffer great pains and even die.

To perform these feats, the shamans put themselves into magical trances by taking hallucinogenic mushrooms, playing sacred drums, singing magical songs, and imitating animal sounds. While in these trance-induced states, the shamans acted out bizarre ritualistic performances in which they leapt high into the air, bent their bodies at odd angles, and occasionally foamed at the mouth. During such rites, the shamans sometimes purposely caused themselves bodily harm, by cutting themselves with knives, swallowing sticks, or eating burning coals.

"A Villain of a Magician"

Although the Siberian shamans had been practicing their rituals for centuries, their activities and feats seriously disturbed the explorers, most of whom were Christians. For example, in 1661, Russian clergyman Avvakum Petrovitch,

A shaman from Siberia's Tungus tribe poses in traditional dress with his drum. The word shaman *comes from the Tungus language.*

A shaman from Mexico's Huichol tribe (right) performs a healing ritual in 1998. Today, traditional shamans continue to practice ancient healing rites.

who was the first person to use the word *shaman* in a published text, consulted with a Tungus shaman in Siberia. This shaman went into a trance, strangled a ram, and twisted off the ram's head in order to predict the priest's future. When Petrovitch wrote his autobiography in 1672, he compared the shaman to a devil, describing the man as "a villain of a magician who calls the demons."[1]

Petrovitch was among the first Europeans to interact with shamans during the age of exploration that marked the seventeenth and eighteenth centuries. By the mid-1700s, European fur trappers, explorers, and priests had encountered individuals performing similar shamanistic practices in Africa, Asia, and the Americas, from present-day Canada, down through Mexico, and into Brazil, Peru, and elsewhere. Like Petrovitch, Spanish, English, French, and other European explorers were shocked and angered by the shamans, whom the Westerners referred to derogatorily

as sorcerers, jugglers, wizards, medicine men, witch doctors, pagans, diviners, and conjurers.

The clash of indigenous cultures with Western values
proved to be harmful to the shamans, who were considered
to be at best crude charlatans, and at worst agents of Satan.
Frightened of the power that shamans had over their people,
European leaders had the shamans murdered or sold into
slavery. This practice continued for centuries. Even in the
twentieth century, the autocratic rulers of the Soviet Union
locked up native shamans in labor camps or executed them.

What Is Shamanism?

Despite centuries of persecution, the practices of the
shamans were never forgotten and remained alive among
the Siberians, Native Americans, and other indigenous
peoples. In the twentieth century, Western anthropologists
began to show a new respect and understanding for the
ancient beliefs of the shamans.

Today, shamans are mainly considered to be healers
who go into trances so they can communicate with spirits.
They use the knowledge imparted to them by these spirits
to effect cures for their patients. These cures are performed
at rituals where the shaman prays, lays hands on the
patient, and extracts diseases through various means.

As in the seventeenth century, however, critics remain.
Some skeptics believe shamans engage in wishful thinking,
feigning ancient wisdom in order to give their lives meaning
in a seemingly meaningless world. Some are even more
severe in their judgment. As Margaret Stutley writes in
Shamanism: An Introduction, "Some writers regard shamans
and their practices as aberrations or frauds, as psychopaths
or as related to hysteria, neurosis and epilepsy."[2] Whatever
the case, belief in shamanism is as ancient as human culture,
with millions of practitioners the world over, and has
remained an important part of many contemporary societies.

Chapter 1

An Enduring Tradition

The practice of shamanism is one of humanity's oldest traditions. Archaeologists have determined that shamans were active at least twenty thousand years ago and were probably common in the earliest human societies that existed one hundred thousand years ago. Although the word *shaman* is linked to the Tungus language of Siberia, the practice of shamanism existed at one time or another in every part of the world. Age-old shamanic techniques continue to be utilized by shamans in many countries today. Millions of people the world over believe in the magical abilities of shamans, who are said to channel cosmic spirits in order to heal the sick, see into the future, and control the physical world through magic. These purported talents remain controversial and unproved, and often run contrary to scientific evidence and the practices of modern medicine. Despite current skepticism, shamans are still found on every continent.

It is unclear why shamanism is common to so many cultures. Some anthropologists speculate that the beliefs materialized spontaneously in different places because there were no cures for the seriously ill other than praying to spirits and experimenting with herbs as medicine. However, since shamanic practices are so similar in widely dispersed cultures, others believe that the knowledge was spread through migration. For example, many anthropologists believe that the natives of Siberia are related to the indigenous peoples of North America. When the Siberians migrated to America ten to twenty thousand years ago, they likely brought their shamanic beliefs to the new continent.

A common bond among shamanic societies supports this theory. They originally were nomadic hunting tribes. Unlike settled agricultural societies where each individual assumes a separate role, such as doctor, political leader, or priest, in hunter-gatherer societies, the shaman took on these roles and more. As Joan Halifax writes in *Shamanic Voices*, shamans

> are in communication with the gods and spirits. . . .
> They are poets and singers. They dance and create works of art. They are not only spiritual leaders but also judges and politicians, [and historians]. . . .
> They are familiar with . . . the ways of plants, animals, and the elements. . . . They are psychologists, entertainers, and food finders.[3]

The First Shamans

While shamans took on many roles, in the mythology of some cultures the first shamans were said to descend directly from the heavens. These healers were the first people— the founders—of the tribe. This is explained by Holger Kalweit in *Shamans, Healers, and Medicine Men:*

> Often the first shaman appeared as a cultural hero and god who brought humanity knowledge from beyond the world. . . . The traditions of primordial shamans reach back to . . . a golden age when gods reigned on earth and . . . helped the first human cultures build their civilizations and societies.[4]

Female Shamans

Although shamanism is often thought of as a male-dominated calling, there have been many female shamans throughout history. As Margaret Stutley writes in *Shamanism: An Introduction:*

> Some [anthropologists believe] that women were the first shamans, and that they appeared in [ancient times] when women were far greater magicians than their male counterparts and also performed important clan functions later taken over by male shamans. This may explain the fact that a number of male shamans practice transvestism [dressing in women's clothing], thereby indicating the former importance of [female shamans]. When a Yakut [Siberian] shaman [performs a ceremony], he dons a woman's headdress and carries a bow. . . . Another view is that a woman was the first human being to receive shamanic powers which she transmitted later to her son who became the first male shaman. . . . [Today there] is a hereditary rite to claim a shaman's function, which may be transmitted in a family equally to boys or girls.

In this drawing, a female shaman beats a ceremonial drum. Some anthropologists believe the first shamans were women.

In Australia, for example, some Aborigines believe that their earliest ancestors were shamans who created the world through dreaming. Present-day shamans in Australia claim that they can travel back to the original epoch in their dreams in order to learn the ways of the first shamans.

In Nepal, the Magar believe that the first shaman lived in a time when there was no sickness, old age, wars, or starvation. Modern Magar shamans continue to invoke the powers of that first shaman, hearkening back to the magical era in order to solve the problems of people in the present day.

Shamanic Beliefs

Shamanic cultures have thrived in many places and shamans are referred to by many names. Among the Northern Paiute of Nevada, shamans, both male and female, are called *puhégem*. In Africa, the Ugandans call shamans *mulogo*, while the Zulus call them *ganga*. In the frozen Arctic regions, the Eskimo consult healers known as *angakoks*. Whatever their name or place of origin, several basic beliefs and practices are shared by all shamans. Shamanic practitioners believe in spirits, both good and bad. These supernatural spirits, which often take the form of animals, can interact with shamans, who control and work with them usually to either benefit individuals or a community. In order to utilize the power of the spirits, shamans induce trances through various means, including intensive drumming, dancing, and singing, or through the use of hallucinogenic drugs.

Another commonality is that shamans channel their trance-induced powers to heal mental or physical illnesses. Shamans may also help those in distress by looking into their future and offering advice. Shamans sometimes benefit their entire community by controlling various aspects of nature, such as to end a drought or flood. A few shamans also use their powers to harm enemies.

Is Shamanism a Religion?

There is conflicting opinion as to whether shamanic practices are based on religion or simply a belief in supernatural spirits. Some believe that shamanism is not a religion because it coexists in many cultures that practice a specific religion and other techniques of magic. As anthropologist and shamanic practitioner Michael Harner explains:

> I characterize it as a method rather than a religion. It is a method which is often associated with a [belief system] known as animism, but distinct from it. Animism is basically the belief in spirits, and spirits are defined in shamanism simply as those things or beings which are normally not seen by people . . . but are seen by shamans in the [shamanic state of consciousness]. . . . So as one . . . keeps seeing, interacting, and talking with spirits, one quite naturally tends to believe in their existence.[5]

Others draw distinctions between shamans and priests because shamans perform their work by utilizing their knowledge of supernatural spirits while priests are called upon mainly to perform rites and rituals.

This distinction was certainly not understood by the first Europeans who encountered shamans, however. These Westerners judged shamans in religious terms, as practitioners of Satanism. The French priest François du Perron wrote in the 1630s of Native American shamans: "All their actions are dictated to them by the devil, who speaks to them now in the form of a crow or some similar bird, now in the form of a flame or ghost, and all this in dreams, to which they show a great deference."[6]

In more recent years, researchers have painted shamanism in a more positive light. Some even speculate that these ancient beliefs—with their standardized rituals, conversations with supernatural spirits, and the faith that deities can effect the lives of mortals—formed the foundations of today's major religions. In this way, the understanding of shamanism can shed light on basic foundations of all societies.

Called by the Gods

The shamanic melding of divine and earthly powers may be seen in the ancient Korean proverb, which states: "Though the gods give shamans their miraculous powers, shamans must learn the technique of invoking them."[7] And in many cultures it is indeed the gods that are said to bestow shamanic powers upon the chosen few. For example, among the Ostyak peoples of western Siberia, shamanism is considered a gift from the sky gods, and a baby must be born with the talent to be a shaman. Those who are related to such a child consider themselves blessed, for they have a shaman in the family who can solicit the spirits on their behalf and protect them from the bad luck and sickness inherent in life.

Not all shamans are thought to be born with the talent, however. Among the Siberian Samoyed, shamanism is inherited. A boy receives the

Pictured is a shaman of the Ostyak people, who believed the sky gods blessed select individuals with the gift of shamanism.

17

powers of shamanism at his father's deathbed by carving an image of his father's hand out of wood. This symbol is said to pass the power of the dying man to his son.

Others come to shamanism spontaneously after experiencing a supernatural vision or after an experience in which a spirit allegedly takes control of them. For example, in the Tungus culture, a person who wants to become a shaman may simply announce that a dead shaman has appeared to him in dreams and wishes the recruit to take on the profession. These so-called freewill shamans are believed to have less power, however, than those who are said to be called by the gods.

Finally, those who have undergone long illnesses, loss of family members, or protracted bad luck may turn to shamanism. These people have hope that communication with the spirits will help alleviate their problems.

In whatever manner an initiate receives the calling to shamanism, it is not necessarily a guarantee that he or she will be able to harness the energy of the spirits. As Native American shaman Lame Deer says of shamanic power: "One can work for it, fast for it, try to dream it up, and yet power does not always come. Not everyone is ready to be the master of power."[8]

Harnessing the Power

Despite such uncertainties, those desiring shamanic powers must often undergo rigorous training and initiation ceremonies before they can hope to communicate with the spirits. The freewill shamans among the Tungus must consort with a devil called Khargi, who instructs them in the ways of the shaman in tension-filled dreams and nightmares.

In some Native American cultures, shamanic powers are also said to be conferred in visionary dreams. Unlike the Tungus, however, these dreams are positive in nature. Nick Downington, a Northern Paiute shaman, describes how spirits arrive in dreams to give a healer power:

Shamanic Initiation

In 1944, Swiss anthropologist Alfred Métraux described shamanic initiation among the Carib tribe of South America. His following account is reprinted in *Shamans Through Time: 500 Years on the Path to Knowledge* by Jeremy Narby and Francis Huxley:

In the tribe of the Caribs of Barama, the master [shaman] takes charge of a small group of students whom he gathers together in a specially constructed hut. He starts by showing them how to make a rattle. He then gives them strong tobacco tea, which plunges them into a trance state during which they visit the land of "water spirits," which they will learn to invoke through magical songs.

Later, after executing frenetic dances under the joint influence of tobacco smoke and [a strong potion of tobacco] juice, the novices enter into a relationship with spirit jaguars. They feel themselves turn into jaguars, walk on all fours, and roar. . . . They run down to the river, scorched and drunk on tobacco juice, to catch fish and worms, so as to ensure the cooperation of aquatic spirits.

Three months of fasting and continence follow these ordeals. . . . The initiation's object is to lead the novice's soul to the beyond. . . . The means deployed to obtain these visions, despite the complexity of their details, are rather simple. They consist above all of ferocious fasts, frenetic dances, and massive absorption of tobacco smoke and juice.

In between dances, the novices sit on a . . . bench. They are completely blinded by the hot pepper that has been rubbed into their eyes, and they listen to their master tell them about the supernatural beings and their attributes. The visions provoked by the intoxication of tobacco juice are naturally very influenced by the mythical tales told by the initiator. Invariably, the candidate believes himself to be transported to the land of spirits.

A man dreams that a spirit of deer, eagle, or bear comes to him. The spirit tells him that he is to be a doctor. When a man first dreams this way he does not believe it. Then the dream comes again. He dreams this way for a long time. The spirit tells him to collect eagle feathers, wild tobacco, a stone pipe, a rattle and other things. When he gets these things he becomes a doctor. He learns his songs [in dreams] when the spirits comes and sings to him.[9]

Other cultures rely less on dreams and more on specific instructions passed on by elderly master shamans. For example, among the Carib of the Amazon rain forest, initiates must undergo months of training in which they have to memorize the names and purposes of hundreds of spirits, the mythology of their culture, tribal genealogy, and a secret shamanic language.

Among the Siberians, shamans cannot practice their work until they have had an independent ecstatic episode. To hasten this event, teenage candidates may take a vision quest in which they hike to an isolated area with no food or water. While there, they allegedly catch animals using only their teeth in order to gain the spirit power of that creature. After returning to the village dirty and disheveled, the initiate might be babbling and hallucinating from hunger. At this time, elder shamans question the recruit and, if satisfied with the answers, begin instructing him or her on shamanic rites.

Initiating a Shaman

Once selected and properly trained, most shamans undergo an initiation rite to confirm their status within the culture. Initiations are usually conducted by elder shamans and consist of a series of difficult and elaborate ceremonies.

Many shamanic initiations are meant to symbolize death of the initiate's previous way of life followed by rebirth as a shaman. Among the Wiradjuri of Australia, an initiate is given a hallucinogenic potion to achieve a trance and then led to a grave filled with snakes and stones said to be magical. The aspirant lies in the grave with the snakes and follows one to the center of the earth, where the snakes infuse him with magical powers. When this is done, the master shaman leads the initiate to a tree where the youngster climbs a rope to reach a bird, called Wambu, that belongs to the Supreme Being. This bird takes the initiate up to the clouds, where shamanic powers are granted to him by the gods.

This belief, that shamans can reach the sky by flying or climbing a rope, is common in shamanic culture. Other methods of accessing the sky include pole climbing, levitation, and even climbing up a rainbow. Among the Niassans of Sumatra, initiates are said to disappear when the spirits take them to the heavens. They are often found several days later sitting in the tops of trees, holding conversations with supernatural beings.

After spending days in the forest during an initiation rite, this shaman of Vancouver's Koskimo tribe appears possessed by a supernatural power.

An ascent to the sky also plays an important role among initiates of the Ojibwa in the upper Great Lakes region of North America. For example, a well-known shamanic tale involves a girl who hears a voice calling her from atop a mountain. She follows a narrow path until she reaches the sky where the Great Spirit gives her a message to heal mankind.

Shamanic Clothes

After shamans are initiated they are allowed to wear the costume of the shaman. Like shamanic techniques, each aspect of the shaman's outfit has a symbolic or magical significance. For example, the entire costume is said to resemble the shaman's universe, with the headdress or cap symbolizing the heavens, the cloak or caftan representing earth, and the footwear taking on the role of the underworld.

To the Ket, indigenous peoples of central southern Siberia, the headdress is the most important piece of shamanic clothing because it is said that the shaman's cap is the center of the shaman's power. Each cap has a decoration—a small iron rod that points outward from a cross-shaped rosette. This antenna-like ornament allegedly allows the shaman to maintain spiritual contact with the heavens. Anthropologist Mihály Hoppál explains:

> If the rosette is a symbol of the universe . . . then the shaman stands at the centre of the world, from where he/she may start the ceremony. In this force-centralizing position, the shaman becomes a go-between the world and the cosmos. . . . The small horn protruding from the cap symbolizes the maintenance of communication with the cosmic forces.[10]

The cap is also decorated with eagle feathers because in Siberia the first shaman in history is said to have been born to a woman who was impregnated by a giant, eaglelike bird. For this reason, eagle feathers represent the awesome powers of that original shaman. Feathers of the eagle and other birds also symbolize the shaman's ability to purportedly fly during his or her rituals.

The cap has a more mundane purpose as well—it protects the shaman's head from the heavy iron crowns that are also part of the costume. There are three types of shamanic crowns, specially made for communing either with heavenly, earthly, or underworld spirits. These may contain symbols such as swords, reindeer antlers, or icons representing other shamanic helper animals. The Manchu shamans of China adorn their crowns with intricately carved decorations such as birds, leaves, and flowers.

Among Siberian shamans, the earthly realm is represented by the shaman's full-length caftan, often made of goat, reindeer, or other animal skin. Like the cap, this tunic is considered to be a symbol of the pathway between the material and the spiritual world. The shamans dye one side of the robe red, to represent spring and day, and the other side black, to symbolize winter and night. Sewn to the dark side are cloth figurines cut to the shapes of dead ancestors, while the light side is decorated with birds and other shamanic animal helpers. The back of the shaman's caftan is embroidered with the world tree, or the tree of life, the branches of which represent the conjoined worlds of the macrocosm, or spirit world, and the microcosm, or human world.

Shamans further decorate their caftans with magical iron symbols representing sacred objects such as animal spirits, the stars, and the sun. In *Shamanism: Archaic Techniques of Ecstasy*, Mircea Eliade describes the iron disks worn by some Siberian shamans:

> In the case of the Yakut, in the center of the back of the caftan, among the disks representing "the sun,"

there is a pierced disk . . . called "the orifice of the sun," but usually it is supposed to represent the earth with its central opening, through which the shaman enters the underworld. The back of the caftan also bears a lunar crescent, as well as an iron chain symbolizing the shaman's power and resistance. According to the shamans, the iron disks serve as protection against the blows of the evil spirit. . . . A fine Yakut shaman's costume . . . must have from thirty to fifty pounds of metal ornaments. It is principally the noise from the ornaments that transforms the shaman's dance into an infernal saraband [song]. These metallic objects have a "soul"; they do not rust.[11]

Other adornments represent body parts. For example, the shamans wear iron bars on their arms to represent arm bones.

The Shamanic Tree

In Siberia, travelers are sometimes asked to sacrifice a few coins or other valuables at a shaman's tree planted along a country road. In *Shamanhood Symbolism and Epic*, edited by Juha Pentikäken, anthropologist Mihály Hoppál explains the meaning of the shamanic tree, and why images of these trees are often embroidered on the back of the shaman's caftan:

The tree is one of the central organizing principles in the world view of the Siberian shaman. . . . They imagined a giant tree—which, for instance, according to the Mongols, grows on the top of a huge mountain reaching the sky. This cos-

mic tree became to the shamans the "road" joining the sky and the earth, the road he has to traverse in the course of a trance. The climbing of the tree represented the ascent of the shaman to the sky. . . .

The tree was a graphic symbol to shamanism, given that it. . . . [joined] through its roots, the lower—underground—dark world with the tree-trunk (the middle world, the world of human beings), with the crown (the upper, the sky world, the world of birds and light, and, ultimately, of supernatural beings). It is a mediator just like the shaman.

Leaves sewn on the chest represent ribs. Large, round disks represent women's breasts, and other ornaments symbolize the heart, the liver, and other organs. Animal symbols are also seen in the shaman's costume. Some wear metallic figures of horses, snakes, birds, lynx, and so on.

Shamans obtain their costumes in several ways. They may have visions of their outfits in dreams or trance states and then set about having them made by local artisans. Others may buy their costume from the family of a dead shaman. Among the Siberians, outfits of deceased shamans are said to be saturated with spirit energy and may shake and tremble while hanging in closets.

A Siberian shaman's costume is decorated with iron disks representing the sun and earth and other ornaments symbolizing the shaman's powers.

In most North American cultures, shamans do not wear specific caftans but paint their faces and bodies with magical symbols. Eskimo wear no costume at all. Instead, they strip themselves naked, except for a special belt worn around the waist. This ritualistic nudity alone allows the shaman to demonstrate his or her powers in a land where temperatures can reach 50 degrees Fahrenheit below zero.

Rattles and Drums

Among Native American shamans, the rattle is another extremely important piece of magical equipment. Rattles made of gourds or dried deer ears are filled with pebbles and are then shaken vigorously throughout most shamanic rites. Among the Shoshone of Nevada, rattles are made from long canes to which small deer hooves are attached. Shamans of other tribes use various instruments depending on their rituals. Hollow wing bones from eagles are fashioned into flutelike whistles. Musical clappers are made from sea shells, oddly shaped rocks, and heavy animal bones.

While rattles are important, the drum is of the utmost significance in all shamanic cultures. Eliade writes:

> [The drum's] symbolism is complex, its magical functions many and various. It is indispensable in conducting the shamanic séance, whether it carries the shaman to the "Center of the World," or enables him to fly through the air, or summons and "imprisons" the spirits, or, finally, if the drumming enables the shaman to concentrate and regain contact with the spiritual world through which he is preparing to travel.[12]

As with all other aspects of shamanic accessories, every aspect of the drum is symbolic, from the materials of its construction to the way it is played. The wooden shell of the drum is representative of the tree of life and the "Center of the World" described by Eliade. To find construction materials for this sacred instrument, the Siberian Samoyed shaman walks into the forest blindfolded and touches a random tree with his or her ax. The shaman's helpers then cut the tree to make the drum shell. By contrast, Yakut shamans inspect hundreds of trees until they find one that has been hit by lightning or has been touched by other perceived supernatural powers.

After the shell has been carved, it must be animated or brought to life through ceremony. Siberian shamans sprinkle vodka, blood, or beer on the shell. Native Americans tell long, involved mythical stories about the purported life of the tree and how the spirits came to choose it for this drum.

The skin of the drum, made from a stretched deer, elk, or other hide, represents the shaman's voice, and it too is carefully selected and animated in a shamanic drum ritual. The skin is then ornamented with pictures of birds, snakes, mythical beasts, magical signs, or other symbols. Tinkling metallic chimes, bells, rattles, and other noisemakers may be attached to the shell. When the drum is finished, it is ready for use in rituals, where it is beaten excessively by the shaman so that he or she may attain the trance state necessary to perform magical rites.

This drum belonged to a shaman of a Nepalese tribe. The drum is the most important tool used in shamanic rituals.

More than Mere Tricks?

Some have argued that shamans are simply like actors whose drums, costumes, and actions convince gullible observers that the practitioner is indeed a powerful magician. This skepticism is disputed by Margaret Stutley, who writes, "Shamanism consists of much more than mere conjuring tricks, for the practitioners themselves are often in deep trance states, the details of which they are unable to recall."[13] The dispute over whether shamans are sophisticated illusionists or truly in touch with the spirit world has remained unresolved. What is true is that shamanism is a calling that many have responded to, and the rites, philosophies, and techniques of the shaman have survived—and are sure to continue—for centuries.

Chapter 2

Communicating with the Spirits

The world in which the shaman lives is filled with supernatural spirits unknown and invisible to most people. These are spirits of animals, insects, birds, rocks, trees, rivers, winds, thunder, the sun, and other natural and celestial occurrences. Shamans believe they can utilize the magical powers of these spirits to help people, to preserve their health, and to cure sickness. It is in this last effort that the shaman is said to be most useful to his or her community.

In order to communicate with the spirits, shamans must enter a trance state, known as a soul flight into the spirit world. To do so, they often take what most people consider to be drastic actions, such as causing self-inflicted pain, creating states of physical exhaustion through drumming and fasting, or taking mind-bending hallucinogenic drugs. Once the trance state is achieved, the shamans experience visions in which they enter into communication with the spirits. The shaman then returns to reality with information purportedly from the spirit that will protect or heal the patient.

During such trance visions, the shaman must maintain control over his or her sanity in order to have the power to contact friendly spirits. These allies will act as guides and helpers on the shamanic journey and protect the shaman from demons and incapacitating spirits.

These aspects of shamanism are undoubtedly among the most controversial. Shamans under the influence of powerful—mostly illegal—drugs, often scream, lurch about the room, babble incoherently, and display other bizarre, frightening behavior. To an outside observer, there is little worthwhile to be found in the advice of drug-addled shamans, or those inflicting pain or physical exhaustion on themselves. Credibility is further stretched when shamans claim they achieve ecstasy and altered states of consciousness from such behavior. However, as Mircea Eliade writes in *Shamanism: Archaic Techniques of Ecstasy:* "The shaman, and he alone, is the great master of ecstasy. A first definition of . . . [shamanism] will be: shamanism = *technique of ecstasy.*"[14]

Techniques of Ecstasy

This term *ecstasy* was first associated with shamanic women, known as Maenads, in ancient Greece. These women participated in orgiastic festivals while worshipping Dionysus, the god of wine. According to Margaret Stutley:

[The Maenads] used alcohol and other drugs to achieve "transformation." They danced in violent abandon on the mountains accompanied by the persistent heavy beat of the tympanum [drum], the eerie smoky light of torches, and their own shrieks and yells. Such intense erotic excitement also contributed to producing the final state of *ekstasis* (standing outside oneself) and *enthousiasmos* (possession by the god). The Maenads saw visions and were endowed with supernatural strength, tearing live animals to pieces and eating the flesh. . . . The animals embodied the god Dionysus, and eating them enabled the eater to . . . attain unity with the deity.[15]

Alcohol continues to play a strong role in the practices of some shamans. For example, powerful Siberian shamans can drink an entire bottle of vodka before going into a trance—an amount that might kill the average person. Other drugs taken by shamans include psychedelic mushrooms, such as psilocybin, which greatly enhance color perception and produce hallucinations along with feelings of ecstasy. Some Native American shamans of the Sonoran Desert induce similar feelings by eating buds from the peyote cactus. In Western cultures, New Age shamans, or neoshamans, use these drugs and may also take the powerful hallucinogen LSD.

Whatever the catalyst, the shaman works with the hallucinations to perform his or her work. This phenomenon is explained by Jean Clottes and David Lewis-Williams in *The Shamans of Prehistory:*

> In these states people believe that they are perceiving things that are, in fact, not really there. . . .

This ancient Greek frieze shows Maenads dancing. The Maenads drank and danced wildly during orgiastic festivals honoring the wine god Dionysus.

Hallucinations may be blissful, ecstatic, or terrifying. In deep states, all the senses hallucinate: People not only see visions; they also hear, smell, and taste non-real things and experience strange sensations in their bodies. These deep states include the condition generally known as trance . . . the state that shamans enter and value so much.[16]

Those who simply experience ecstasy under the influence of drugs, however, are not considered shamans. In order to perform their purported healing rituals, shamans must enter trances where their souls are said to leave their bodies.

A female shaman of Siberia's Teleut tribe dances and drums around a fire in this nineteenth-century drawing.

Shamans can also achieve altered states of consciousness from physical means, such as prolonged periods of
intensive drumming, dancing, and singing. According to
the 1904 writings of anthropologist Weldemar Bogoras,
shamans of the Chuckee culture in Siberia drum for

> several hours, during all which time the shaman
> exercises the most violent activity without scarcely a
> pause. After the performance he must not show any
> signs of fatigue, because he is supposed to be sus-
> tained by the "spirits" themselves. The degree of
> endurance required for all this . . . [can] be acquired
> only by long practice.[17]

In whatever manner shamans achieve altered states,
their soul flight tends to unfold in similar steps. During the
first phase, the intense pain or initial fright of the experience is said to be a symbolic dismemberment of the body.
As this stage passes, the shaman enters a period of ecstasy
said to be a physical renewal of the skin and internal
organs. The next stage involves soul travel to the sky, where
the shaman converses with the spirits and discusses the reasons he or she needs their advice. Next, the shaman dives to
the underworld, where the souls of dead shamans are consulted. Finally, the shaman is able to formulate a revelation
and return to reality, where he or she can use this unique
information to help the client on whose behalf the journey
had been taken.

During soul flights, shamans undergo physical changes
to the body and mind. At the beginning of the experience,
the shaman's heart races and sweat pours from the brow.
At these times, the shaman may laugh hysterically or
shriek and yell madly. During the final stage of the experience, the shaman may fall to the floor in what is known as
a cataleptic trance, where the muscles are rigid, the pulse is

nearly indiscernible, and the shaman looks dead to observers.

The Vision Quest

While drugs and drumming can be used to invoke trance states, some shamans, particularly Native Americans, use intense bodily deprivation to bring on altered states of consciousness. This is achieved during what is called a vision quest, whereby the shaman exhausts his or her body and mind to an extreme degree.

When a shaman undertakes a vision quest, he or she walks to an area in the wilderness to spend several days alone. No food or shelter is taken, and none is to be searched for in the wild. At best, vision seekers must fend off mind-numbing boredom; at worst, they are exposed to great perils, including wild animal attacks, storms, lightning strikes, excessive thirst, hunger, and even madness. These dangers are forgotten when the deprived shamans have visions that connect them to the spirit world. One such vision was described by Dick Mahwee, a Paviotso, or Northern Paiute, shaman from western Nevada who spent several days in a cave as a young man, listening to bears and mountain lions hunt through the night. Finally, Mahwee saw the spirit of a tall thin man holding an eagle feather. The spirit instructed him on ways to become a shaman, saying:

> I have this feather in my hand. You must get feathers like it. You are also to find the things that go with it. Get dark beads. Put them on the quills of the feathers and tie a strip of buckskin to the quills. Also get a hoof of a deer, and down from the eagle. With these you can go to your people to cure them. These are the weapons against sickness. You must get three rolls of tobacco. You can use them to tell

your patients what made them sick and then you can cure them. The tobacco will also help you if you are choked with clots of saliva when you suck out the disease. Bathe in the water at the foot of the cliff and paint yourself within . . . [white paint].[18]

Such visions often occur after shamans deprive themselves of food and drink for extended periods of time. Some shamans claim to have superhuman strength and endurance during such fasts. For example, Pedro de Haro, a shaman from the Mexican Huichol tribe, claims to have completed five-day vision quests with no food or water—a feat that might kill an average person.

Power from the Spirit of the Night

According to Paviotso shaman Dick Mahwee, his powers are derived from a mysterious force called the spirit of the night. His description of this spirit is detailed in *Shamanism in Western North America* by Willard Z. Park:

The Indian doctor gets his power from the spirit of the night. This spirit is everywhere. It has no name. There is no word for it. The Indians hold this spirit so sacred that they are afraid if they had a name for it the spirit would be angry. No one has ever given it name.

Eagle and owl do not give a shaman power. They are just messengers that bring instructions from the spirit of the night. Some doctors have [spirits that live in water holes called] water-babies for their messengers. . . . They do not give him his power; they only carry messages from the spirit of the night. When the shaman is treating a patient he calls for the water-babies and they bring him instructions from the spirit.

At the time that the spirit of the night gives power for doctoring, it tells the shaman to ask for help from the water-babies, eagle, owl, deer, antelope, bear or some other bird or animal.

When shamans get their power it always comes from the night. They are told to only [heal the sick] at night. This power has nothing to do with the moon or the stars.

While on such quests, shamans might also induce altered states of consciousness through intense, self-induced pain such as putting their hand in a roaring fire or lying on an anthill swarming with stinging ants.

Although scientific explanations for visionary phenomena are limited, Holger Kalweit offers his theory:

> [As] a result of malnutrition and vitamin deficiency, fundamental changes [take] place that [are] conducive to visionary experience. . . . Self-mortification [self-inflicted pain], too . . . heightens the possibility of visions, for through it, large quantities of adrenaline and [other compounds] are released, which influence consciousness.[19]

An Inuit shaman's mask depicts the flight of a shaman's soul to the spirit world during a trance.

These extreme physical changes wrack the body. However, the brain, deprived of the energy it needs to function properly, may produce hallucinations and visions. As Kalweit writes, the shaman "is suddenly endowed with extrasensory perception, precognition, the ability to leave his body, to see spirits, and the like. He has received attributes of sacred existence and has himself become a messenger, an epiphany of holiness. . . . [He] manifests a higher world."[20]

Dreamtime Experiences

While vision quests allegedly provide great knowledge, a shaman will usually only pursue this dangerous and draining power perhaps less than a dozen times in his or her life. On a regular basis, shamans may turn to their dreams, which are also considered a source of useful visions.

Shamans have dreams like those experienced by everyone else, but because they are attuned to the spirit world, shamans also have visionary dreams, called big dreams. These might repeat themselves the same way over the course of many nights, or they may be so unusually vivid that the shaman feels as if he or she is awake. During such dreams, shamans believe that they are communicating directly or indirectly with their personal spirits called guardians or power animals. These big dreams are not interpreted for mystical meaning or symbolism but are taken as literal step-by-step instructions from the guardian.

The Australian Aborigines have a particularly profound relationship to shamanic dreams. In the mythology of the Aborigines, the world was created by cosmic shamans who dreamed people, plants, and animals gave them all the life force. When Aborigine shamans want to gain power, they tap into the "dreamtime" force of the original creators by traveling, while they sleep, to what is called the Otherworld. An elderly Aborigine shaman, Allan Balbungu, referring to himself in the third person, describes how he induces his soul to leave his body while dreaming. During this soul flight, he makes the journey to the Otherworld, where he learns powerful shamanic dances:

The Bizarre World of Trance

Shamans perform their magic while in a deep trance, often caused by hallucinogenic drugs or exhaustive drumming and dancing. In *The Shamans of Prehistory*, Jean Clottes and David Lewis-Williams describe this altered state of consciousness:

> [Shamans] find themselves in the bizarre world of trance: Monsters, people, and settings are intensely real. . . . With one's eyes open . . . hallucinations are [geometric shapes] . . . projected onto surrounding surfaces. Western subjects liken these projected images to "pictures painted before your imagination" and to "a motion picture or slide show." They seem to float across walls and ceilings. At the same time, the surfaces themselves become animated. A picture hanging on a wall, for instance, will be seen in three dimensions and with heightened colors, and it may start to move, to come alive. In [this state] people feel that they can fly and change into birds or animals. People no longer simply "see" strange things; the things become part of their hallucinations. . . .
>
> One of the most frequently reported experiences of . . . [shamanic] altered consciousness is transformation . . . into an animal. A Westerner experiencing an altered state said, "I thought of a fox, and instantly I was transformed into that animal. I could distinctly feel myself a fox, could see my long ears and bushy tail, and by a sort of introversion felt that my complete anatomy was that of a fox."

[The shaman] thinks of nothing but the dances he has seen [in dreams] and his soul keeps going back to the spirits to learn more and more about the dances. His wife may then notice that his soul has been leaving the body every night, and she will say: "Why do you always leave me?" But the shaman will tell her that he goes to the spirits to learn dances. . . . His body lies quietly sleeping. But under the leadership of the helping spirit others come up from the underworld and take possession of the shaman's spirit. . . . They tear the soul to pieces and each spirit carries a piece to the underworld. There, deep under the earth, they put the shaman's soul back together again. They show him dances . . . and sing songs to him.[21]

After Balbungu has taken this journey, he shows the dances to the members of his tribe. They paint their bodies with white stripes, which represent the skeletons of their dead ancestors, and perform the dances as Balbungu sits in a tree and sings ecstatic songs that he says the spirits taught him. As this happens, Balbungu and the dancers fall into a trance and all are transported to the dreamtime Otherworld of the shaman.

The Powers of the Animal Spirits

Whether through dance, dreams, vision quests, self-mortification, or drugs, the goal of all shamans is to commune with the spirits. Since most shamanic cultures evolved from hunter-gatherer societies, a plethora of these holy deities are related to the animals, which these ancient societies depended upon for food, clothing, and other necessities. As Tom Cowan writes in *Shamanism as a Spiritual Practice for Daily Life:*

Our ancestors depended on animals for much of their material life. Animals provided food, clothing, ornamentation, tools, weapons, medicine, shelter, transportation, and companionship. They acted as harbingers of seasonal change, danger, and fluctuations in the weather.

Compared to human beings, animals collectively possess greater strengths and powers. In the animal population we find individuals who can run faster; swim better; see, hear, and smell more accurately; climb rocks and trees faster; hunt more successfully; and of course, fly. . . . Many animals live longer and are physically stronger than we are. Some animals survive in environments too harsh and inhospitable for human beings, such as deserts, bottoms of lakes and oceans, and in chambers bored deep into the Earth.[22]

For these reasons, shamans have always attempted to draw powers from animal spirits. Through their trances and rites, shamans absorb the wisdom and connect with these forces of nature unavailable to most people.

This Stone Age rock painting from Africa shows a shaman dancing around an elephant. Animal spirits play an important role in shamanism.

Among North American shamans, the eagle is one of the most potent symbols. The Inuit believe that the eagle represents the Supreme Being, who first introduced feasting, music, and the drum to their culture. Shamans purportedly derive their magical abilities from eagles along with other powers including courage, grace, balance, speed, strength, wisdom, excellent eyesight, knowledge from hard work, and the ability to glean little-known healing methods. It is also said that the eagle can lift a shaman up in its powerful claws and rise to great heights, visiting the sky and the spirits that live there.

In Siberia, the bear is held in similar esteem. Only the strongest shamans may commune with bear spirits. Those who do so have bear images of cloth, metal, and other materials hung above their beds and over the doors of their homes. These are decorated with ribbons, beads, leather fringe, and other artistic elements believed to hold power. Bear shamans might also have bones, dried paws, teeth, or claws from a dead animal.

A shaman of the Apsaroke people wears an eagle body as a headdress. Eagles are a powerful symbol in American Indian shamanism.

While bears are an obvious symbol of strength, no creature is too small or insignificant to convey shamanic powers. For example, the wisdom of the praying mantis allegedly allows shamans to manipulate time. Communing with ants provides patience and stamina.

The snake, or serpent, which is feared and reviled in many cultures, is another extremely important animal to shamans. Some Aborigine shamans say that they can fly through the air on the backs of serpents. In one part of Australia, shamans claim to climb up to the sky using the reptile like a rope, pulling themselves hand-over-hand up the creature's back to the heavens. Among Mayan cultures in Central America, it is believed that a snake can pass along its wisdom by inserting its forked tongue into a shaman's mouth.

The Antelope Charmers

A clear example of shamans gleaning knowledge from helpful animals may be seen in the traditional hunting practices of the Paviotso of North America. The antelope is a particularly important animal to this culture, and the animals migrate through the Paviotso homeland in early spring when winter food supplies are exhausted. When this happens, the tribe calls on the antelope shaman who will take charge of the hunt.

When the Paviotso are ready to begin an antelope drive, the shaman conducts a trance ritual that allows him or her to take possession of the antelope spirit. This permits the shaman to act as an antelope and become what is called an antelope charmer. With the wisdom of the antelope, the shaman consults dreams and trances in order to tell scouts where to find the animals grazing. Once the scouts report back with the news of antelope packs, the shaman oversees the construction of a corral made from ropes of sagebrush bark.

The night before the drive, the shaman holds a special dance while wearing a mask made from an antelope head. Music is played on a notched stick, which is rasped with a rattle, while the shaman sings until daylight, calling out to the antelope in a language that the animals purportedly understand. At dawn, the Paviotso hunters set out to drive the antelope herd into the corral. If the antelope charmer has done his job properly, the antelope will be docile when corralled.

Although most Paviotso shamans focus on healing the sick, the antelope charmer is unique. As Willard Z. Park writes in *Shamanism in Western North America:* "Antelope-charming . . . is the one well-recognized function of the shaman which is not a part of the all-pervading belief in curing. In fact, it is the only important shamanistic performance of the Paviotso that is not heavily charged with beliefs about the cause and control of disease."[23]

The Master Animals

In some cultures, a shaman can only gain wisdom from animals through an intermediary who allows the exchange to occur. In Colombia, shamans of the indigenous Tukano tribe must deal with a supernatural red dwarf known as the Master of Animals, or Vaí-maksë. To contact this intermediary, the shaman takes hallucinogenic drugs and travels to the Milky Way, the home of the Master of Animals. The master does not work for free, however, and the shaman must knock on the spirit's celestial door and make a bargain with food or medicinal herbs to obtain help. After an agreement is reached, the Master of Animals lets the shaman into his abode. Gerardo Reichel-Dolmatoff describes the interior of the dwarf's home in *Shamans Through Time: 500 Years on the Path to Knowledge:*

> Inside, along the wall and on the rafters and beams, innumerable animals are crouched as if asleep. In the corner several [animal spirits] are sitting, somnolent and with hunched shoulders; jaguars and snakes are lying on the floor, and brightly colored birds sit on the rafters. . . . The [shaman] fills two

large baskets with certain species of game animals and carries them to the door.[24]

These animals offer advice or instruction to the shaman for healing the sick or harming tribal enemies.

Brother Moon

While shamanic practices revolve around animal spirits, shamans also draw wisdom and power from the heavenly bodies. For example, ancient Inuit stories speak of Brother Moon, who controls the moon's movements. It is said that the moon is where the souls of animals and people go to live after they have died.

This shaman's mask represents Brother Moon, an Inuit deity that shamans called on to cure disease and to make game animals plentiful.

Inuit shamans believed that epidemic diseases were caused by Brother Moon. Lunar eclipses, therefore, foretold of an imminent epidemic. To avert this disaster, the shaman of the traditional Inuit conducted séances to communicate with Brother Moon, asking the spirit how the epidemic could be prevented. In most of the old tales, Brother Moon asked for animal sacrifices, prayers, dances, and other offerings.

Brother Moon is also said to control the availability of game animals. When an animal, such as a caribou, was scarce, shamans flew up to the moon to obtain news as to the migration patterns of the animals. The shaman also made offerings and if these pleased Brother Moon, the spirit might give the shaman a caribou to take back to Earth. The shaman then released the animal in the wild, where it reproduced and made the species plentiful again.

Similar beliefs concern the sun, major stars, and planets in the night sky. But there are many things that can serve as power spirits for shamans. Examples include water, thunder, and mountaintops. There are also spirits purportedly in less-obvious things such as the night, morning mist, the blue sky, and the four directions, east, west, north, and south. Guardian spirits may also be found in people and their body parts (including hands, feet, and sexual organs). Ghosts, graves, and the body parts of the dead, such as teeth and bones, are also sources of power. In other words, almost anything on Earth can, in the view of shamans, contain guardian spirits.

Chronic Mental Illness?

To some, the spirit powers, hallucinations, and trances of shamans represent nothing more than antics of people who are crazy. As psychologist and shamanic authority Richard Noll states:

The "Strong Eye"

When the shaman is in a trance, he or she may develop an intense gaze known as the strong eye. This allegedly allows the shaman to see for great distances and understand things that are inexplicable to the average person. In 1924, explorer Knud Rasmussen describes the strong eye as used by young Inuit shamans who lived along Canada's Hudson Bay. Rasmussen's description is reprinted in *Shamanism: An Expanded View of Reality* edited by Shirley Nicholson:

[The strong eye] consists of a mysterious light that the shaman suddenly feels in his body, inside his head, within the brain, an inexplicable searchlight, a luminous fire, which enables him to see in the dark, both literally and metaphorically speaking, for he can now, even with closed eyes, see through darkness and perceive things and coming events which are hidden from others; thus he looks into the future and into the secrets of others.

The first time a young shaman experiences this light . . . he sees far ahead of him, through mountains, exactly as if the earth were one great plain, and his eyes could reach to the end of the earth. Nothing is hidden from him any longer; not only can he see things far away, but he can also discover souls, stolen souls, which are either kept concealed in far, strange lands.

It had long been believed by many scholars that shamans suffered from chronic mental illness. That is, that the bizarre experiences that they report were nothing more than the ravings of florid psychotics, and that the "primitive" societies in which they lived were too ignorant to recognize such psychopathology and instead institutionalized it into a religious social role.[25]

Other nonbelievers say that shamans are simply illusionists whose drug-addled antics contain little spiritual value. Whatever the case, shamans claim to be able to travel to otherworldly places to obtain knowledge beyond the understanding of most people. If this is a fantasy or a reality, only the shaman knows for sure.

Chapter 3

Healers

In the annals of tribal myth and magic, shamans have been known to perform a variety of rites, including bringing luck to hunters or death to enemies. But the shaman's main occupation in most cultures has been to prevent illness and to heal the sick using the combined skills of a doctor and the cosmic miracles of a magician. Before the advent of modern medicine, the work of the shaman was one of the most important jobs in any society. Today, shamans still use ancient remedies to heal and give comfort to believers.

Healing is based on the belief that sickness is caused by several problems. In some cultures it is said that illness is a crisis with the patient's soul, which may have been kidnapped by evil cosmic forces or simply wandered off. The shaman treats this condition by either finding the soul, capturing it from an enemy who stole it through shamanic magic, or otherwise inducing it to return to the patient's body.

In other shamanic societies, illness is blamed on the victim's soul having been possessed by evil spirits. In such cases, shamans perform rites to drive off the harmful force. These cures can be extremely complicated. As Mircea Eliade writes:

> Only the shaman can undertake [cures] of this kind. For only he "sees" the spirits and knows how to exorcise them; only he recognizes that the soul has fled, and is able to overtake it, in ecstasy, and

A Child's Shamanic Healing

Maria Sabina was a shaman of the Mexican Mazatec tribe. Born in 1894, Sabina took psilocybin, or sacred mushrooms, at a very young age. During the ensuing ecstatic trance, she claims that they told her how to find the herbs that cured her uncle's sickness. In 1977, she told her story to Joan Halifax, who related it in *Shamanic Voices*:

I was eight years old when a brother of my mother fell sick. He was very sick, and the shamans of the [area] that had tried to cure him with herbs could do nothing for him. . . . So I went to take the sacred mushrooms, and I brought them to my uncle's hut. I ate them in front of my uncle, who was dying. And immediately the [mushrooms] took me to their world, and I asked them what my uncle had and what I could do to save him. They told me that an evil spirit had entered the blood of my uncle and that to cure him we should give him some herbs, not those that the [other shamans] gave him, but others. I asked where these herbs could be found, and they took me to a place on the mountain where tall trees grew and the waters of the brook ran, and they showed me the herb that I should pull from the earth and the road that I had to take to find them. . . . I took them, I brought them home, I boiled them in water, and I gave them to my uncle. A few days later, the brother of my mother was cured.

Under the influence of psilocybin mushrooms, the Mazatec shaman Maria Sabina (right) learns which herbs will cure her sick uncle.

return it to its body. Often the cure involves various sacrifices, and it is always the shaman who decides if they are needed and what form they shall take; the recovery of physical health is closely dependent on restoring the balance of spiritual forces. . . . Everything that concerns the soul and its adventure, here on earth and in the beyond, is the exclusive province of the shaman.[26]

Skeptics say that such beliefs stand in stark contrast to the known causes of sickness, including hereditary factors, infections, viruses, and other problems. Shamans explain away modern medicinal cures by saying that infections and other physical problems are obvious symptoms of a damaged or missing soul. Shamans, therefore, concentrate on the patient's spiritual and mental state, believing doctors are only doing half the job by exclusively treating the body. Those seeking middle ground point out that spiritual pursuits, such as prayer or meditation, have been shown to improve the health of some patients.

Calling Back the Soul

Such debates matter little to those in rural areas where modern medical treatment is not an option. Among the indigenous peoples of Siberia, when a person falls ill, a shaman is asked to call the soul back to the patient's body. In the Teleut culture, to perform the necessary ceremony, a shaman lays the patient down on a rug in the middle of his tentlike house, known as a yurt. In a typical chant for an ill child, the shaman will say to the soul: "Come back to your country! . . . to the yurt, by the bright fire! . . . Come back to your father . . . to your mother!"[27]

A shaman of the Siberian Buryat culture adds some props to the chant. The shaman's patient will lay still with several magical objects placed around the body. One of these talismans is an arrow with a red silk thread tied to it. The thread runs out the door of the yurt, with the other end attached to a limb of a birch tree. It is believed that the patient's soul will return to his or her body by traveling along this thread and entering into the yurt. To entice the soul into the tent, the family of the patient will have arranged offerings of tobacco, cakes, and liquor. Outside, the shaman's assistant holds onto a horse because it is said that the animal can sense the return of the soul before humans and will quiver as the wandering soul approaches. Again, the chant plays an important role in the ceremony. To an adult male, the shaman might say:

> Where are you lingering, whither have you gone? . . . Your wife and dear children, so unexpectedly orphaned, call you hopelessly weeping and wailing, and cry to you, "Father where are you?" Hear and have pity on them, come back to them. . . . Your herd of countless horses longs for you, whinnying loudly and crying pitifully, "Where art thou, our master? Come back to us!"[28]

If the soul refuses such entreaties, or is unable to return because it is lost or imprisoned in the underworld, the shaman must search for it. To do so, the shaman will conduct a ceremony in which he or she enters an ecstatic state. This may require the shaman to drink large quantities of alcohol or take psychedelic mushrooms while beating on a drum and singing for hours. After the shaman has achieved ecstasy, his or her spirit will abandon the body in order to travel through the woods, over the mountains, or even to the bottom of the ocean in search of the patient's soul. While making this cosmic trek, the shaman will encounter various other spirits, both good and bad, and question them in order to ascertain the whereabouts of the patient's soul.

If the shaman finds the soul, he or she will grasp it tightly in hand and, after awaking from the trance, return it to the patient's body by pushing it in through the right ear.

Traveling to the Underworld

If the shaman cannot find the soul, it is assumed that it has been kidnapped and imprisoned by the Lord of the Underworld, known as Erlik among the Buryat. In such cases, the shaman must make difficult and dangerous sacrifices to Erlik to gain the soul's release.

Sometimes Erlik demands another soul to replace the one in question. The shaman and the patient must then pick an enemy whose soul can be used in the trade. To obtain the soul, the shaman purportedly turns into an eagle and swoops into the victim's yurt while he is sleeping. The eagle tears out his soul and takes it to the underworld, where Erlik accepts it in trade. Under these circumstances, the patient is said to recover while the victim soon dies. The reprieve is only temporary, however. The Buryat believe that when a soul is deliberately stolen in this manner, the original patient will die in either three, seven, or nine years.

Not all soul retrieval is so violent, and helpful spirits can be used to recover souls that have been stolen. For example, shamans of the Siberian Ostyak tribe travel to the underworld with a bear spirit. When the shaman finds the stolen soul, the bear frightens the thief into loosening its grip on the soul. The helper bear then catches the soul and returns to Earth with it.

After a shaman enacts such a cure, he or she traditionally spends hours recounting to the audience in great detail the hardships and dangers of the journey. And because battling with sprits of the underworld is so treacherous, shamans often suffer as much as their patients. Yakut shaman instruct observers to tie them up so spirits will not carry them off during the battle for a soul. During the healing séance, the shamans shake violently, hiccuping, grunting, and shrieking with hysterical and terrifying sounds.

Sucking and Singing Doctors

While many shamans depend on prayers and spirit travel, others enact cures that are much more physical in nature. For example, Native American shamans often advise that a patient take a series of sweat baths in extremely hot saunas and then dive into an ice-cold river or lake to alleviate sickness.

While sweating has been shown to cure fevers and other minor ills, many shamans use a much more controversial practice of "sucking" the illness out of the body. This is based on the belief that disease is caused by pieces of bone, crystal, or other foreign objects that enemies or witches have surreptitiously placed within the patient's body. In 1976, a Yurok Indian named Dewey George described how sucking doctors work: "They press their mouth on your belly; they'd suck. I saw a doctor suck out a big ball, round [golf-ball sized], and it had roots coming down from it. I guess it was cancer."[29]

Among the Miwok in California's Sierra Nevada, sucking is the most common type of shamanic cure. The sucking doctors wear elaborate costumes, which include abalone shell necklaces, animal hair, feathers, bird skulls, and body paint. Craig D. Bates describes the work of Miwok sucking shamans in an essay in *California Indian Shamanism:*

> Very powerful individuals, [sucking doctors] usually cut the affected area and sucked out the cause of disease, often manifested as bits of wood or bark, a stone, coffee berries, a sizzling black [volcanic] rock . . . a flicker tail feather, a hummingbird's beak, claws of a martin, a fish bone, a metal nail, a worm

or even a piece of knotted . . . string. A sucking doctor might sometimes use a small bone whistle, made of red-tailed hawk or owl wing bone, and blow and suck the whistle over the affected part without cutting. When the whistle was plugged up, the doctor sucked the cause of the sickness out of the whistle. . . . One woman shaman, upon removing a black, sizzling, rough stone from the back of a young girl who had been poisoned by another shaman, told the girl there would be times in her life when her back would still hurt her. She assured the girl that she could always be cured by calling again up the shaman whether [the shaman] was dead or alive.[30]

These bone and fiber figures found in Utah are symbols of sickness. American Indian shamans purportedly cured sickness by sucking it from the body.

How to Become a Sucking Doctor

Shamans among the Miwok Indians have claimed to cure patients by sucking diseases—often manifested in the form of a rock or piece of bone—out of their bodies. In *California Indian Shamanism* (edited by Lowell John Bean), Craig D. Bates describes how a young boy might gain the power to become a sucking doctor:

> Sometimes a Central Miwok boy sucked up a polliwog or another sort of strange, small black object from the water four times with a hollow stick. Many boys played with hollow reeds, but only a few caught such things. Afterwards he told no one what he had done, but went home, went to bed, and dreamed that he could cure people by sucking. He might then go looking for sick people, and would become known as a doctor after he had cured a sick person. He had little power as a boy, but by the time he was 20 or 25 he would become a powerful doctor.

The Miwok are also among the tribes who employ singing shamans to heal the sick. These doctors sing songs learned from spirits while stroking or otherwise manipulating the patient's body. In the 1970s, an unnamed modern doctor explained singing shamanism, stating: "When the doctor sings, it's like he's snake charming. The pain gets hypnotized by the songs and starts rising in the body to see what it is and . . . the doctor can take it out . . . with his hands."[31]

Among the Kumeyaay in Southern California, some singing shamans specialize in curing the bites of rattlesnakes. These singing snake shamans sing a low chant and stroke the patient while holding a feather. Days later the patient is purportedly cured. Ethnographer Lowell John Bean, who has witnessed such a treatment, offers this explanation for the success of the therapy: "Modern medical science recognizes that rattlesnake venom kills by stopping the heart. The shaman, by slowing the heart beat, effectively slowed the movement of the venom through the body, thus preventing fatally large amounts of venom from reaching the heart at one time."[32]

Dancing Doctors

The Miwok are also familiar with dancing doctors, shamans who cure by performing ritual dances. These shamans do not apply herbal cures or suck disease, but instead perform slow, deliberate dances in which each step is full of spiritual meaning. A dancing shaman will prepare for the healing ceremony up to ten days before the performance. To cleanse their spirits, they abstain from sex and follow special diets, avoiding meat. Some fast for extended periods of time.

When the ritual is to be performed, the dancing shaman dons ceremonial regalia, which includes a woodpecker-tail head plume, an eagle-claw necklace, and a cape made from hawk tail feathers. Using a ritualistic medicine bow and arrow that cannot harm the patient, the dancing shaman shoots at the source of the pain while dancing. The shaman might also shake a rattle and drive off the pain using a whistle made from bird bone.

Before such cures are performed, the shaman must be paid. In past centuries, common forms of payment were deer meat, cloth, or shell money, known as wampum. If the patient died, the shaman returned the payment, but assumed no responsibility. If too many of a shaman's patients died, however, he or she was assumed to be under the influence of evil spirits and might be murdered by members of the tribe.

Herbs That Teach Lessons

Even if most patients recover, there has been a long-standing debate over the true value of shamanic cures such as sucking, singing, and dancing. There is less dispute over the tradition-al shamanic practice of healing with herbs and plants.

Shamans that utilize herbal medicines have long assumed the roles of doctors, nurses, and pharmacists among believers. Unlike modern medical practitioners, however, these shamans believe that the cure is not in compounds found within plants, but in the spirits that live in the plants. As one unnamed shaman in the Amazon rain forest said, "The spirit of the plant must come to you in your dreams . . . [and tell you] how to prepare it and what it will cure."[33]

Sometimes the visions of plants can be a guiding force in a shaman's life. For example, Oglala shaman Black Elk, who was born in South Dakota in 1863, had a vision of a plant when he was only nine years old. This unusual plant had flowers of four different colors. He had a second vision of the plant about ten years later, and decided to hunt for it. After a prolonged search, he found the plant with flowers of blue, white, red, and yellow growing in a dry gulch. Before picking the plant, Black Elk made an offering of red willow bark to it. Then he said to the herb, "Now we shall go forth . . . but only to the weakest ones, and there shall be happy days among the weak."[34]

Black Elk believed that the herb called to him at that time because he needed it the next night when a young boy became very sick and could not walk. Although Black Elk had never cured anyone before, he went to the boy's tepee and smoked a medicine pipe, passing it around to the patient's relatives. The shaman summoned the healing thunder gods by making rumbling sounds on his drum because the instrument was said to stimulate the minds of the listeners, making them feel closer to the mysterious healing spirits.

As the ceremony proceeded, Black Elk began to improvise. He instructed the virgin sister of the sick boy to sit by his side. He asked for a cup of water. Finally he offered a prayer:

My Grandfather, Great Spirit, you . . . have made everything, they say, and you have made it good and beautiful. . . . The two-leggeds [people] on earth are in despair. For them, my Grandfather, I send a voice to you. You have said this to me: The weak shall walk. In vision you have taken me to the center of the world and there you have shown me the power to make over. The water in the cup that you have given me, by its power shall the dying live. The herb that you have shown me, through its power shall the feeble walk upright. From where we are always facing (the south), behold, a virgin shall appear, walking the good red road, offering the pipe as she walks, and hers also is the power of the flowering tree. From where the Giant lives (the north), you have given me a sacred, cleansing wind, and where this wind passes the weak shall have strength. You have said this to me. To you and to all your powers and to Mother Earth I send a voice for help.[35]

Black Elk, a nineteenth-century Oglala shaman, had a vision in childhood of a plant that proved to have great healing powers.

After the prayer, Black Elk chewed the herb and spit pieces of it over the boy and in the four directions. He gave the water to the sister to give the boy to drink and left the tepee. According to Black Elk, the boy was cured four days later and lived to be thirty years old.

The Healing Power of Foolishness

Not all work performed by shamans is solemn and serious. According to Oglala shaman Black Elk, happiness encourages shamanic healing powers. He described one such shamanic ceremony to John G. Neihardt in *Black Elk Speaks*:

[Thirty] heyokas [shamans], one for each day of a moon, were doing foolish tricks among the people to make them feel jolly. They were all dressed and painted in such funny ways that everybody who saw them had to laugh. [A shaman named] One Side and I were fellow clowns. We had our bodies painted red all over and streaked with black lightning. The right sides of our heads were shaved, and the hair on the left side was left hanging long. This looked very funny. . . . Each of us carried a very long bow, so long that nobody could use it, and it was very crooked too. The arrows that we carried were very long and very crooked, so that it looked crazy to have them. . . .

Even while we were singing [serious shamanic songs], the heyokas were doing foolish things and making laughter. For instance, two heyokas with long crooked bows and arrows painted in a funny way would come to a little shallow puddle of water. They would act as though they thought it was a wide, deep river that they had to cross. . . . One would then plunge into the shallow puddle head first, getting his face in the mud and fighting the water wildly as though he were drowning. Then the other one would plunge in to save his comrade, and there would be more funny antics in the water to make the people laugh.

Herbs That Heal

Shamanic doctors like Black Elk often have knowledge of thousands of plants. In addition to seeing plants in dreams, some shamans experiment with herbs, searching for curative powers within them. They collect plants and use them to make teas or to make washes to bathe wounds. Herbs can also be made into poultices, which are soft, moist masses of herbs, usually heated, spread on cloth, and applied to an aching or inflamed part of the body.

There is often disagreement, however, as to whether herbal cures are real or fraudulent. As anthropologist Dorothy Cator wrote in the early twentieth century about shamans in Borneo: "For fever, some of the native doctors have splendid medicine; but on the other hand many of them are awful [imposters], and ascribe every kind of magical power to some absolutely rubbishy concoction, and charge accordingly."[36]

While Cator's words may be true in some cases, many herbs and plants utilized by shamans have real healing value. For example, researchers at Harvard University have shown that shamans in the Amazon rain forest use over thirteen hundred species of plants that have value as medicines, poisons, or narcotics. Mark J. Plotkin is an ethnobotanist—a scientist who studies the use of plants by indigenous peoples. In his book *Tales of a Shaman's Apprentice,* he talks about gathering medicinal plants with a Yanomami medicine man called Jaguar Shaman:

> We stopped at a large liana, a woody vine that curved and twisted its way skyward. . . . The medicine man indicated that he valued the sap of the liana's stem as a cure for children's fevers. . . . [The plant] is rich in alkaloids . . . widely used for their sedative and muscle-relaxing effects. . . . These species play important roles in modern medicine. [A compound found in liana] has been used by Western physicians since the 1950s to treat glaucoma, myashenia gravis (weakness of the skeletal muscles . . .), and postpartum heartburn. And extracts of another species provides L-dopa, an amino acid in use since the late 1960s to treat Parkinson's disease.[37]

In addition to the medicines mentioned by Plotkin, a full 25 percent of modern drugs are made by refining plants that have been used by Amazonian shamans. These include hydrocortisone, used to treat inflammation, reserpine for

A Peruvian Indian climbs a tree with a liana vine wrapped around it. Valued by shamans, liana compounds are also used in modern medicine.

nervous disorders, digitalis for heart failure, and quinine for malaria.

Powerful Outsiders

While shamans cure the sick and comfort the community, most attempt to live apart from the people they heal. As John Lee Maddox writes in *The Medicine Man:*

> [The shaman] holds himself aloof from the other members of the tribe; he lives in a house different in structure from those of the common people; as a rule he does no laborious work, but is supported by his fellows; he eats a special food; he paints his body, masks his face, and does many things [such as taking drugs] that would be considered "sinful" for

an ordinary individual to attempt. . . . All of these peculiarities tend to heighten his influence, and . . . serve to increase his control over people.[38]

Such actions have led to accusations by outsiders that shamans enrich themselves by preying upon the superstitions and weaknesses of the sick. Despite the doubts, people who study indigenous shamans believe that most of these healers are honest and have complete confidence in their methods. As anthropologist M.H. Kingsley writes about shamans in Africa: "It would be difficult to see why they should doubt their own methods, because, remember . . . the majority [of their patients] recover."[39]

Like any other profession, a few shamans might be imposters, while the majority do their best to help alleviate suffering. Believers point out that even twenty-first-century medicine cannot cure all diseases and that the shaman has long played a valid and important role in the annals of healing.

Chapter 4

Evil Shamans

While shamans are usually associated with healing, some shamanic practices are reportedly capable of causing harm. Shamans calling on malevolent powers use the same techniques as healers—entering ecstatic trances, consulting with spirits, and utilizing herbal concoctions. Instead of curing the sick, however, these powers are used to seek vengeance. The lessons of the spirits are used to cause psychological harm and inflict illnesses such as cancer and heart disease. Common herbs are used as poison.

While accusations of sorcery and poisoning by shamans are often based on ancient superstitions, these beliefs persist in some shamanic societies today. As Ekkehart Malotki and Ken Gary write in *Hopi Stories of Witchcraft, Shamanism, and Magic:*

> [People in shamanic cultures] have an abiding fascination with magic and supernaturalism, and with everything that transcends rational explanation. . . . Thus, in the [shamanic] worldview, tradition, myth, legend, and historical accounts can be equally valid records of experiences and are often woven together in mythology and in rituals, where the spoken or sung word is held sufficient to "magically" cause the desired results.[40]

As a result of this elevated interest in the supernatural, the deeds of evil shamans practicing witchcraft still hold great power even in the modern world. And this deep and abiding fear of "black magic," or witchcraft, is so ingrained in the human psyche that even in the most modern nations, certain segments of society continue to fear its practitioners despite nonbelievers' attempts to debunk such beliefs.

Witch Shamans

Why shamans decide to use their powers for evil is a matter of debate. Since shamans regularly battle evil spirits, it is said that malevolent spirits may sometimes triumph over the healer. Such defeat may turn the shaman into a force of evil. Other beliefs stipulate that some extremely powerful shamans get their strength from evil spirits. This is true for shamans among the indigenous peoples of Greenland. These shamans may use these ill-gotten powers for good or bad, as they chose.

The freedom to use evil powers to effect good is not a universal belief, however. Among the Apache of Arizona, witch shamans are rarely considered to have positive qualities. Instead, those who use their power for dark acts are equated with aberrant behavior, as Morris E. Opler writes in *Apache Odyssey: A Journey Between Two Worlds*:

> There is a conceptual link between the idea of witchcraft and wantonness, sexual aberration, and incest. It is assumed that no one but a witch would be likely to be a sexual deviant or commit incest. Witches are described as carrying on their practices in a naked or half-naked condition and indulging in lewd gestures or acts.[41]

While the Apache believe that walking the path of evil is a personal choice, the Ga in Guinea believe that witch shamans are born, not made. In such cases, children are believed to be cursed from birth, having inherited demon spirits from their mothers or dead relatives. The Hopi of

In past centuries, Arizona's Hopi people believed that Canyon de Chelly was the Home of the Sorcerers, where kidnapped infants were taken by evil shaman to learn witchcraft.

Arizona, on the other hand, believe that evil shamans will try to kidnap innocent children and attempt to turn them into witches. This is done by a shaman who—twenty days after a baby is born—disguises himself as a fly, buzzes into the parent's home, and magically picks up the victim. The child is then said to be carried off to what is called the Home of the Sorcerers in Canyon de Chelly. Here the infant is initiated into the ways of witchcraft at a secret meeting place deep underground.

After receiving the demon spirits, the children are returned to their homes. When they grow up, the resulting witch shamans are conscious that they have been corrupted against their will. Although they perform malicious acts, they attribute their evil deeds to the demon spirits that possess them. In *The Heathens: Primitive Man and His Religions*, William Howells maintains that the possessed shamans have the option of performing good deeds with their demonic powers of the possessing force. Howells writes:

The demon is not necessarily bad, and may even be used for curing, or knocking down trees, but if he once is put to evil he is like a shark that has tasted blood, and he will force the [shaman] he lives in to kill neighbors against his or her will, and with no ordinary motive, and may actually kill the [shaman]. . . . In fact, one is usually possessed against her will, and makes a struggle against it. The victim pines away, goes through mental anguish, and may develop a real psychosis. The demon usually triumphs, of course, and the newly fledged witch then resigns herself to the fact.[42]

Malevolent Deeds

In whatever manner they become evil, witch shamans have been blamed for all types of bad luck within a community, from the withering of crops to the deaths of babies. Believers say sorcerers are capable of stealing souls, especially those of innocent children, which can result in incurable sickness in the victim. Sometimes the souls are said to be eaten by the witch shaman, slowly, so as to cause the victim the most prolonged pain. Demon-possessed shamans may also steal a victim's luck or cause women to become sterile by stealing their wombs.

Malevolent shamans can attack individuals in a variety of ways. In Greenland, it is said that witch shamans use magic to create an evil spirit or ghost, called a *tupilak*, that kills enemies. It is made from herbs and plants; the bones, fur, and skin of animals; and pieces of cloth stolen from the intended victim. The shaman uses a magic chant or song to bring the creation to life. In *Shamanism*, Merete Demant Jakobsen describes the creation of a *tupilak*. According to an unnamed witness, the shaman, working on a beach, "packed half a [shirt] sleeve with hair, grass, and mosses and mumbled over it. . . . [The shaman told it to] transform and become a *tupilak*, a ghost, and straight away it sprang into the water."[43] By diving into the sea or a river, the *tupilak* can easily find its way to the intended victim since most Greenlanders live along the nation's habitable coast lands.

In some traditionalist African cultures, the witch shaman may send his or her spirit to kidnap the victim's soul, or possibly the spiritual essence of a vital organ, such as the liver or heart. According to Howells:

> [The evil soul] sails through the air like a fireball, and must be directed by the owner, since it cannot find the target alone and must have him pointed out. This means that [evil] cannot travel very far, and so the [shaman] is usually somebody within the village; and the man who is fearful that he is under attack can go into temporary hiding at a little distance.[44]

While individuals may be able to hide from a witch shaman, sometimes the evildoers target an entire community. The malefactors are said to call up millions of pests such as grasshoppers, cutworms, mice, or kangaroo rats to destroy crops. Witches may also control the clouds and the weather in order to create droughts or floods that destroy crops and cause famine. Among the Hopi it is said that witches use horrible smells to cause clouds to disappear. According to Ekkehart Malotki and Ken Gary: "Offensive odor is often used to make the clouds recede. Consultants relate stories of witches blowing their breath at the clouds through the malodorous bone of a diseased human corpse, or bending over, sticking their naked buttocks directly towards the clouds, and blowing through their spread legs."[45]

The Poison Doctors

Perhaps the most feared of the malevolent shamans are those who use poison to harm their enemies. Among the traditionalist California Miwok, these men and women are referred to as poison doctors, or *tu yu ku*. They are capable of concocting deadly substances from various poisonous plants as well as snake, toad, or other animal venom. These are mixed with hair or other items from the victim.

Poison doctors might mix their potions with other items meant to bring bad luck, such as dried rattlesnake heads, ground human bones, body parts of bears or other animals, and the ashes of burned abalone shells. Once concocted, the poisons are administered in various ways. The evil powder can be spread surreptitiously around a home, buried nearby, or sprinkled in the path the victim often walks. Some poison doctors use stinging red ants or centipedes to spread their toxins. Others put their concoctions on pinlike items such as sharp plant stems, cactus needles, or feather or porcupine quills. These can be jabbed into the victim or, through magical means, sent sailing like a poison dart over long distances. When the latter method is employed, the poison doctor is said to shout out the name of the victim and command the dart to pierce the head,

This carving represents a tupilak, an evil spirit created by witch shamans in Greenland used to attack their enemies.

breast, or other body part of the intended target. Whatever the method, poison doctors allegedly cause their victims to die. Depending on the potency of the toxin, some pass away immediately, others after suffering through long, painful illnesses.

The Miwok believe that poison doctors inherit their trade from their parents. To gain the powers necessary, they eat minute amounts of poisonous plants. This also grants immunity to the toxins, and therefore the poison doctors can work with them without fear.

Fear of poison doctors was so strong among the Miwok that they devised rituals to avoid becoming targets. For example, when a woman cut her hair, she buried it in a secret hiding place so the poison doctor could not use it in a poisonous formula. The fear was so strong that the Miwok were careful to root out a poison doctor from the tribe before any misdeeds were done. This forced the poison doctor to operate in secret. Once services were needed, the

Harsh Treatment for Witch Shamans

While the indigenous peoples of Greenland respect shamans, they deal harshly with those who use their powers for malevolent ends. In 1888, anthropologist Gustav Holm described the punishment doled out to witch shamans called *Ilisitsok*. His story is quoted in *Shamanism* by Merete Demant Jakobsen:

[The shaman] can be an Ilisitsok without performing the actions [of a witch]; but if he does, he runs the danger of becoming mad, talking deliriously. . . . If this happens he is bound with his hands and feet straight on the platform or the floor and gagged. He will get nothing to eat or drink, and sometimes a big stone is placed on the chest of the ill person. He will lie like this until he dies. This remedy is so incorporated in the consciousness of the native that it is used without the presence of [a healing shaman to oversee it]. Often the torments are shortened as the ill person, after having been tied up, is thrown into the sea. The only way that a patient can be freed from this treatment is if he admits that he is an Ilisitsok and mentions the crimes, either real or imagined, that he has on his conscience, after which he cannot continue as a Ilisitsok.

poison doctor used stealth to carry out the evil acts. Even after the task was accomplished, the malefactor had to hide guilt—especially if the victim died. As Craig D. Bates writes: "To avert suspicion, the poison doctor cried and grieved more than anyone for the one he killed."[46]

Charm Dolls and Bodily Substances

Poison doctors and other malevolent shamans can use harmful herbs in less direct ways. In what is known as imitative magic, herbs and other nefarious potions can be stuffed into effigies or dolls. These dolls imitate or resemble the victim and may be used for evil spells. The most well-known example of this sort of black magic is voodoo dolls, which are made of wood, wax, clay, or rags. (The shamanic versions of these effigies are misnamed because they have nothing to do with the Haitian voodoo religion, which does not condone black magic). Shamanic dolls have been found in cultures from ancient Egypt to present-day South America. Traditionalist shamans in Native American tribes, including the Menominee, Iroquois, Seminole, and Pueblo, have also utilized effigy magic.

A shaman with evil intent uses an effigy as a focus for a black magic spell in which malevolent thoughts can be concentrated on the doll. After this is done, the shaman may jam a needle into the doll, allegedly transferring the pain to the intended victim. These dolls are believed to be more powerful when they contain something from the designated victim's body, such as toenails, hair, sweat, saliva, and urine.

Even without the use of an effigy doll, substances and body parts taken from human bodies can be used for insidious purposes. In *The Night Has a Naked Soul*, Alan Kilpatrick illustrates this ghoulish scavenging:

> In ancient Mexico Aztec sorcerers highly prized the severed left forearms of women who had died in

Dressed in the magical clothing hanging on the left, these shamanic charm dolls were used in rituals to cause an enemy harm.

childbirth as potent weapons to cripple, paralyze, or otherwise anesthetize their victims. In a similar vein Cherokee conjurors favored collecting the moist saliva of their victims. . . .

In northeastern Oklahoma [witch shamans] were rumored to keep an assemblage of strands of hair taken from various animals and from humans. Using these extracted follicles, these witches could then transform themselves into the exact shape of the hair's owner.[47]

Werewolves and Raven Mockers

The belief that shamans can disguise themselves as animals or birds is widespread. Among the Hopi, malevolent shamans are said to assume the shapes of coyotes, wolves, foxes, nighthawks, bats, or even domestic pets such as cats and dogs. Shamans may also turn themselves into horrifying monsters. Traditionalist Cherokee, for example, believe that a witch can assume the shape of a werewolf. Among the Navajo, the practice of taking on such a form is known as shape shifting.

The owl is another form assumed by shape-shifting shaman, and the Cherokee word *tsi:sgili*, is a term for both the hoot owl and witch. According to one unnamed source, the owl is both "hated and feared because it was held to be the commonest form into which witch [shamans] transform themselves."[48]

Evil shamans are also believed to be able to transform into cannibalistic vampires. These shamans are said to gain power by feeding on the blood, entrails, and hearts of living humans. To do so, they fly into a victim's house, lift them from the bed, throw them to the floor, and torture them by eating them slowly. These horrific vampires are known among the Cherokee as raven mockers, James Mooney writes, because "withered and old . . . [the fearsome birdlike creature] flies through the air in fiery shape, with arms outstretched like wings, and sparks trailing behind. . . . Every little while as he flies, he makes a cry like the cry of a raven."[49]

Hopi shaman vampires are said to be able to extend their lives for four years by pulling out the heart of a relative. They do so by inserting a corkscrewlike instrument known as a spindle into the victim's chest. After this horrific act, the heart is taken to the Home of the Sorcerers, where it is stored in a box specified for this purpose.

A Spider's Web That Kills

In the 1930s, anthropologist and author Morris E. Opler lived with an Apache shaman whom he gave the pseudonym "Chris." In *Apache Odyssey: A Journey Between Two Worlds*, Chris explains to an old woman with stomach problems that she has been made sick by a witch:

Some time ago you had trouble with some woman. . . . You had a party and there were women there. I will describe the dress of this woman, but I will not call her by name. You will remember this woman and the place, and you will know how it is. There was a dark-complexioned woman, not very tall, with a blue skirt and a blouse, black with white dots. And her swinging sleeves were red. She had a little red ochre on her face, and she had no grey hair. This woman asked you for a drink of corn beer. You did not look at her. You passed drinks to all the men who were present and to some of the women, but to her you didn't give a drink at all. You thought you did, but you missed her. . . .

Under her hand this woman had a spider's web, one of the strongest and most dangerous witchcraft weapons of all. This spider web represents the ropes of the sun. It is black, blue, white, and yellow. That spider's web is wrapped around your arms and legs. It is not a very pleasant thing to show you, but it is a killing thing, because the sparkling of the web is the fire that is eating you, and she meant it to hold you till you were down in the bed wasting away.

The Negative Effects of Drugs

While science cannot explain men turning into raven mockers, the use of hallucinogenic drugs by shamans often results in bizarre behavior and paranoia. It is conceivable that weird events blamed on witches may be an outgrowth of these negative drug experiences. At the beginning of the twentieth century, on the Mescalero Indian Reservation in New Mexico, dozens of Apache tribespeople began taking peyote to attain shamanic powers. This presented a problem because in earlier times a single shaman alone held power within the tribe. His visions and communications with the spirits were respected by all. The fact that many Apache were now taking the drug prompted rivalries and called into question a shaman's mystical status. As L. Bryce Boyer, Ruth M. Boyer, and Harry W. Basehart write:

The use of peyote by other people at ceremonies made its psychological and physiological effects common, and the uniqueness of the shaman's experiences disappeared. The peyote meetings became places in which shamanistic rivalries and witchcraft flourished. Disruption resulted, rather than cohesiveness through shared experience. . . . [Antagonisms] became so open and bloody that eventually the peyote gatherings were abandoned. The hostilities which became overt during the meetings were ascribed to the peyote. Since its use involved witchcraft practices, its ingestion was equated with the potential for witchcraft.[50]

The Apache shamans stopped using peyote around 1910. In the early 1960s, however, there were several men still living on the reservation who had taken part in the earlier ceremonies and were still using the drug. A shaman known as Ancient One continued to perform witchcraft and was said to have killed many people, both Apache and tribal enemies, by supernatural means. Even his children

Although shamans have long used hallucinogenic drugs like peyote (pictured) to induce trance, some shamans used these drugs as a tool of witchcraft.

were said to be afraid of him. The reasons he continued to use peyote for nefarious means were unknown. The Boyers and Basehart surmise that "[the Ancient One] could demand greater recompense and command greater respect from performing rituals which were . . . illegitimate in Apache practice and belief."[51]

Similar problems have occurred among the Yanomami people who live in the Amazon rain forest. Traditionally, Yanomami men take several psychedelic drugs, collectively known as *ebene*. These drugs are placed in long hollow tubes and one man blows the drug up another man's nostrils. The recipient typically chokes, gasps, grimaces, and rubs his head with both hands. His eyes begin to water and his nose runs so profusely that long strands of green mucus drip from each nostril. Sometimes the man falls to the ground, stunned, vomiting, and convulsing with dry heaves.

Although this experience seems quite unpleasant, it allegedly allows the men to converse with supernatural spirits known as *hekura*. At the beginning of the experience, the man sings soft songs and has a pleasant dialogue with the spirits. As the *ebene*'s effects take hold, however, this conversation can turn into loud screams, wild gesticulations, and arguments with the spirits. Sometimes these experiences turn violent, and the man, said to be possessed by evil *hekura*, will cast negative spells on his enemies. On occasion the possessed Yanomami will even attack someone physically, with fists, a machete, a club, or poison arrows. Peruvian shaman Fernando Payaguaje insists that it is the degree of drug intake that is responsible for the violence and corruption:

Some people [take drugs] only to the point of reaching the power to practice witchcraft; with these crafts they can kill people. A much greater effort and consumption of [drugs] are required to

reach the highest level, where one gains access to the visions and powers of healing. . . . Shamanism affirms life but also spawns violence and death. The beauty of shamanism is matched by its power—and like all forms of power found in society, it inspires its share of discontent.[52]

Armed with a machete, this Yanomami shaman under the influence of psychoactive substances presents a deadly threat.

"Witches Are Easy to Believe In"

While belief in witch shamans is less common in the twenty-first century, the ancient fear of supernatural curses remains in some cultures. As Alan Kilpatrick writes, "Although belief in . . . 'Raven Mockers' has been somewhat curtailed by the electronic monsters seen on today's television

Injuring Through Object Intrusion

There is a widespread belief in shamanic cultures that a malevolent shaman can injure someone by allegedly inserting a foreign object into the victim. In *The Night Has a Naked Soul*, Alan Kilpatrick examines some of these beliefs:

> The magical technique of inserting an injurious, foreign object into a victim appears to vary widely. . . . In ancient Mexico the Nahua-speaking Aztec believed that their "owl men" [witch shamans] enjoyed the power to cast spells mentally into the bodies of their victims, which would then materialize as sharp fragments of bone or obsidian. During the seventeenth century the Huron Indians were evidently troubled by witches who could perform similar feats of magic. . . .
>
> Apparently, not all "object intrusion" was accomplished by mental projection. . . . [Vengeful] sorcerers in Melanesia were known to infect their victims by using a "ghost-shooter," a type of bamboo blow-gun containing the ground bones of a corpse, leaves, and other unidentified by-products. . . . Even more astounding is the Yagua conjurer of Peru who . . . carries within his body a host of lethal darts that he can extract from his skin . . . and, if provocation warrants it, hurl into the body of his victim.

Evidently, it was commonly held that a sorcerer could harm a victim from a considerable distance. An extreme case of this belief appears to have existed among the Creek Indians during the nineteenth century. [According to anthropologist John R. Swanton:] "They firmly believe that their Indian enemies have the power of shooting them as they lie asleep, at a distance of 500 miles. They often complain of having been shot by a Choctaw or Chickasaw from the midst of these nations."

screens, some apprehension still persists among the Cherokee communities in northeastern Oklahoma about the plausible existence of these folkloric predators."[53]

Of course, skeptics have long dismissed witch shamans, attributing belief in their alleged powers to uneducated people who need something to blame when things go wrong for unknown reasons. There may be other forces at work as well. Alleged victims of malevolent shamans engender great public sympathy. It is possible that they are simply making up stories to either gain the support of their neighbors—or to direct negative attention to an enemy by making false accusations. Such charges also allow people to blame evil spirits for the ills of their society and use the alleged witch shaman to absorb their hatred. As William Howells writes:

> [With witchcraft] a tribe can gather and impute to [the shaman] a number of recognized evil desires and emotions, and so make the witches serve as a horrible example; witches are easy to believe in, and witchcraft can be hated communally, so that it makes a bond; and for these reasons and because it is beyond the pale it makes a safe shooting gallery in which to expand the floating hatred present in a group.[54]

In every society there are members who feel powerless, and so they practice malevolent shamanism in order to achieve power. When inexplicably bad things happen to good people, it can usually be blamed on evildoers. Whether they are using supernatural means or regular methods of violence to inflict pain matters little to the victims.

Chapter 5

Shamans in the New Age

Shamans are usually associated with traditionalist cultures whose beliefs in shamanism date back thousands of years. People in most Western societies, such as Europe and the United States, have long dismissed shamanism as superstitions practiced by primitive cultures. In the United States, beginning in the nineteenth century, Native American shamanistic beliefs were strongly suppressed by government authorities interested in Christianizing and Americanizing Indians on reservations. Throughout most of the twentieth century, the original shamans in Siberia were brutally oppressed by the government of the Soviet Union. In the 1920s, however, a newfound respect for the shamanistic belief system began to emerge among scholars and researchers. As Jeremy Narby and Francis Huxley write, "Anthropologists began listening closely to shamans and recording what they said about themselves. This is when the understanding deepened."[55]

Despite interest within the scientific and intellectual communities, shamanism remained an esoteric subject for decades. This changed in the late 1960s, when millions of middle-class Americans began to experiment with hallucinogenic drugs—some of the same ones used by shamans for thousands of years. Many of these drug users were seeking spiritual enlightenment and believed that psychedelic drugs unleashed powers of the mind which heretofore had been hidden from most "civilized" people. These powers included shamanic feats such as foretelling the future, conversing with the spirits of plants and animals in vision quests, and healing with herbs and other ancient methods. In *Shaman's Path*, Joan B. Townsend explains:

These trends were characterized by the search for a new meaning in life, which began to find its expression in a feeling of kinship among all people, a "back to the land" movement, and the valuing of simple, "natural" lifestyles and convservationist concerns. Significantly, there was also a strong

In 2004 a shaman performs a ritual in Ecuador. Over the past several decades, shamanism has experienced a revival around the world.

interest in nonorthodox theologies, especially spiritualist, mystical, and Eastern religious philosophies, as well as Native American culture, including shamanism.[56]

The Teachings of Don Juan

In the midst of this era of renewed interest in shamanistic spirituality, Peruvian-born author and anthropologist Carlos Castaneda published a book that popularized shamanism as never before. *The Teachings of Don Juan* details Castaneda's relationship in the early sixties with a *brujo*, or desert sorcerer, named Don Juan Matus. Guided by this mysterious Yaqui Indian sorcerer, Castaneda becomes a sorcerer's apprentice, ingesting a variety of drugs including jimsonweed (called "devil's weed"), peyote (referred to as "mescalito"), and a mixture of secret herbal ingredients known as "little smoke."

Don Juan says that one of these plants will become Castaneda's "ally" and help him see the world as a sorcerer sees it. Under Don Juan's guidance, Castaneda takes several drug trips in Mexico. Castaneda does not glorify drug use, however. In fact, many of his experiences bordered on madness. As biographer Charles Carreon writes:

> To use the devil's weed, [Castaneda hallucinated that he] had to catch two lizards, sew one's eyes shut, and then stitch closed the mouth of the other, to set up a situation where one lizard could see, the other could talk, and thus the information known to the first lizard could be communicated to the initiate. To use mescalito was easier, but [under its influence, Castaneda imagined that he was] urinated [on] by a Mexican dog possessed by the spirit of the psychedelic cactus while [Don Juan] laughed

himself sick. And inhaling the little smoke sounded like about as much fun as parachuting into [a parallel universe] without a compass or a return ticket. . . . [Castaneda hallucinated that he was] being strafed by a horsefly the size of a house.[57]

In addition, Castaneda allegedly turned into a crow and fought a battle for his very soul with a witch. In 1965, after suffering through more bizarre experiences, Castaneda became too frightened to continue. When *The Teachings of Don Juan* was published in 1968 at the height of the psychedelic hippie movement, however, the book became an instant bestseller. Castaneda followed his success with a series of books written in turgid, nearly indecipherable language about several wizened old sorcerers who performed miraculous acts of magic while under the influence of mushrooms and peyote. Eventually, Castaneda sold 8 million books, and an untold number of hippies took long hikes into the deserts of Arizona and Mexico to seek shamanic powers under the influence of peyote and mushrooms.

Although Castaneda spawned what has come to be called a neo-shamanistic movement, there are serious doubts that his books are based on real anthropological study. On a Web site concerning Castaneda, Cecil Adams explains:

Experts pointed out that Don Juan's "teachings" bore little resemblance to actual Yaqui Indian religious beliefs. Hallucinogenic mushrooms didn't grow in the Sonoran Desert, where Don Juan supposedly lived. Anyone who'd gone walking for hours in the desert at the hottest time of the day, as Castaneda claimed he and Don Juan had done, would surely have died of sunstroke.

A Crack Between Two Worlds

In 1968, at the height of the counterculture revolution, Carlos Castaneda published *The Teachings of Don Juan*. Coming at a time when millions of people were experimenting with psychedelic drugs, Castaneda's words were voraciously consumed by people seeking spiritual enlightenment. In the following passage, Yaqui Indian sorcerer Don Juan explains to Castaneda how to find the doorway to the spirit world:

> The particular thing to learn is how to get to the crack between the worlds and how to enter the other world. There is a crack between the two worlds, the world of the [sorcerers] and the world of living men. There is a place where the two worlds overlap. The crack is there. It opens and closes like a door in the wind. To get there a man must exercise his will. He must, I should say, develop an indomitable desire for it, a single-minded dedication. But he must do it without the help of any power or any man. The man by himself must ponder and wish up to a moment in which his body is ready to undergo the journey. That moment is announced by prolonged shaking of the limbs and violent vomiting. . . . When the convulsions do not stop the man is ready to go, and the crack between the worlds appears right in front of his eyes, like a monumental door, a crack that goes up and down. When the crack opens the man has to slide through it. It is hard to see on the other side of the boundary. It is windy, like a sandstorm. The wind whirls around. . . . Once on the other side, the man will have to wander around. His good fortune would be to find a helper nearby—not too far from the entrance.

The precisely rendered dialogue, which lends credibility at first, has the opposite effect when the books are read in succession—no one could have accurately recorded so much talk without a tape recorder, which Castaneda says he was forbidden to use. Don Juan's manner changes from book to book. In *Teachings* he is stern, but in later books that cover much of the same time period he makes jokes and uses English colloquialisms, even though Castaneda says he spoke only Spanish. . . . [One researcher] prepared timelines of the first three books showing that their events couldn't plausibly have occurred in the order stated.[58]

When skeptics asked Castaneda for proof, none was provided by the author. While some experts dismissed Don Juan as a fictional character, others defended Castaneda's books and said they remain essential to those who wish to learn about shamanism. As Michael Harner writes in *The Way of the Shaman:* "The books of Carlos Castaneda . . . have performed the valuable service of introducing many Westerners to the adventure and excitement of shamanism and to some of the legitimate principals involved."[59]

Beyond Castaneda

Even as Castaneda was popularizing the concepts of shamanism, a new generation of anthropologists was traveling the globe searching for traditionalist shamans in their native lands. Unlike researchers of an earlier age, these anthropologists were not content to be mere outside observers. Instead, they wanted to apprentice themselves to shamans and learn their methods firsthand. That meant trekking through dense, dangerous jungles after taking mind-bending psychedelic drugs.

In the 1960s, Harner apprenticed with Jivaro and Conibo Indian shamans in the Amazon rain forest. While learning shamanic concepts, he ingested a mysterious drug known as "little death", made from the ayahuasca vine. Although he heard beautiful singing and had fascinating hallucinations, the drug trip was filled with horrors. Harner writes:

> I was completely certain that I was dying and that the bird-headed people had come to take my soul away on [a] boat. . . . [My] body slowly began to feel like it was turning to solid concrete. I could not move or speak. . . . Simultaneously, my abdomen seemed to be turning to stone, and I had to make a tremendous effort to keep my heart beating.[60]

After these feelings had passed, however, Harner found himself communicating with dinosaur-like, reptilian creatures: "The creatures showed me how they had created life on the planet. . . . I learned that the dragon-like [spirit] creatures were thus inside all forms of life including man. . . . We humans were but the receptacles and servants of these creatures."[61]

This experience changed Harner's life, and in the early 1970s, he began teaching shamanic methods in the United States. He was soon recognized as an authority on practical shamanism—that is, shamanic techniques that could be learned simply and easily by almost anyone. In 1980, when he published *The Way of the Shaman*, it was lauded as a foremost resource and reference on shamanism and a pioneering catalyst of a modern neo-shamanism movement. As he contends:

The ayahuasca vine produces a hallucinogenic substance ingested by Amazonian shamans to induce visions.

[Before 1980, shamanism] was rapidly disappearing from the planet as missionaries, colonists, governments, and commercial interests overwhelmed tribal peoples and their ancient cultures. . . . [Now]

shamanism has returned to human life with star-tling strength, even to urban strongholds of Western "civilization," such as New York and Vienna. . . . There is [a] public . . . rapidly-growing and now numbering in the thousands that has taken up shamanism and made it a part of personal daily life.[62]

In 1985, Harner took another step to promote shamanism among a wider audience, setting up the Foundation for Shamanic Studies (FSS) in Mill Valley, California. Through the FSS, Harner provides lessons in shamanic belief to more than five thousand neo-shamans every year and oversees more than two hundred shamanic training programs in North America, Europe, Latin America, and Australia. Although Harner has experimented with drugs in shamanic settings, his discipline is strictly drug free. Trance states are achieved through drumming, chanting, and meditation techniques such as deep, rhythmic breathing.

Anthropologist Michael Harner studied with Amazonian shamans and opened the Foundation for Shamanic Studies in California in 1985.

"Practical Guidelines to Use Spiritual Power"

Classes taught by Michael Harner and others connect neo-shamanism with basic shamanic traditions. For example, neo-shamans believe in an alternate reality, different from the daily world, where the basic physical laws of nature do not apply. In this alternate universe, spirits of plants, animals,

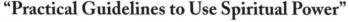

A shaman in Peru uses soft drinks and liquor to perform a ritual. Neo-shamans often break with traditional practices and devise their own rituals.

dead ancestors, and monsters may all mingle with a Supreme Being. Like traditional shamans, neo-shamans believe that these spiritual beings can teach them lessons if they can be contacted while the shaman is in a trance state.

While there are similarities with ancient shamanic belief, neo-shamanism also differs in some significant ways. Traditionally, shamans were associated with a specific culture, tribe, or group. Neo-shamans, however, usually act as individuals and are not often associated with a church, organization, or cult. As Joan B. Townsend writes, shamanic groups

> are actually little more than agglomerations of people who come together in workshops and in local meetings. These groups are amorphous, rarely have a formal structured membership, and are comparatively short-lived. People often participate in a number of these kinds of groups simultaneously, one of which may emphasize neo-shamanism, one healing, one psychic development, and one spiritual seances.[63]

In another break with traditionalism, neo-shamans do not follow set rituals and beliefs that have been passed down from generation to generation. Instead, they might pick and choose among a mélange of methods, incorporating, for example, fortune-telling with tarot cards, healing with quartz crystals, or meditation. Neo-shamanists also tend to pursue spirituality outside of traditional Western religions such as Christianity and Judaism. As one unnamed woman attending a neo-shamanic workshop writes:

> I don't have religious beliefs except that any route to enlightenment is fine. Spirituality is what counts, not religion. Also I believe that if a person has knowledge and power, these should be used to help/teach/guide/pleasure others. . . . Shamanism [gives] you some practical guidelines to use spiritual power.[64]

Neo-Shamanistic Healing

Whatever the motivations of the neo-shamans, their knowledge and interpretation of ancient healing techniques is in demand as growing numbers of people who have mental or physical illnesses consult with shamans to seek cures. These people turn to neo-shamans for a number of reasons. There are those to whom doctors cannot offer a cure. Other patients are afraid of invasive surgery or being injured by mistakes made by medical practitioners in a hospital. Still others seeking neo-shamanistic healing have problems with the side effects or expense of pharmaceutical drugs.

To effect cures for such patients, neo-shamans, like their traditional counterparts, do not concentrate on tumors, coughs, or other symptoms of disease. Instead, they study the patient's attitudes, emotions, and spiritual outlook. Physician and neo-shamanic healer Larry Dossey writes:

> [The neo-shaman] needs to know what the illness means to the patient—what the illness is "saying"; what occurred in the life of the patient prior to the onset of the illness; how the patterns of many elements of the world (sun, moon, stars, weather, plants, animals, other humans) correlate with the

In 2000 a Mongolian shaman performs an exorcism to drive out the evil spirits that have taken control of a young man.

happenings in the patient's life. These kinds of questions are almost never a part of the modern doctor's quest for cure; but it is essential that [neo-shamans] know something of them before proceeding.[65]

Once these issues are determined, the neo-shaman will effect a cure by chanting and praying, asking patients to "visualize" themselves as cured, and using hypnosis or other trance-inducing techniques. This may be coupled with herbal healing and instructions on purifying the body with saunas, vegetarian diets, and other cleansing regimens. In describing the importance of diet, neo-shaman Lewis E. Mehl claims: "We learn to listen to our bodies after eating. Was that food in harmony with what was needed? Or did it bring cacophony to the body's song."[66]

What sets this apart from traditional shamanism is that many neo-shamans use their healing systems in concert with modern medicine. As Mehl writes, he has no problem with "using penicillin and [herbal medicine] together, or using visualization and surgery together. The idea is to combine the good medicines that work so that each can be more effective."[67]

Neo-Shamans in Many Fields

While modern physicians scoff at such attitudes, the use of alternative medicine, including neo-shamanism, is on the rise. Although they are few in number, neo-shamans work today in hospice care, psychiatric inpatient facilities, drug and alcohol treatment settings, outpatient mental health, medical hospitals, juvenile treatment facilities, and even in a few school systems. For example, Myron Eshowsky worked for six years openly practicing shamanism in a psychiatric setting at the Mental Health Center in Madison, Wisconsin. As Eshowsky writes:

In my years there, there were hundreds of opportunities to apply ancient knowledge to modern problems. Most of the clients were poor, of varied cultural background, many experiencing extremely traumatized lives, and exhibiting severe emotional difficulties with little resources internally/externally to effect change.

Many came from awful histories. It was not uncommon that they had long histories of treatment without success. Some had migrated from the streets of Chicago to get away from the violence. Some were [escaping genocide in] Cambodia. Many had stories of physical, sexual, and emotional abuse, and neglect in childhood. . . . It was never my intention to introduce shamanism into the mental health center. What began as a seed blossomed into a fertile testing ground. Staff were referring more and more clients to me even though I did not talk with anyone there about what I was doing nor about the results I was having until I was about to quit.[68]

Neo-shamans such as Eshowsky treat problems including obesity, addictions, depression, low self-esteem, and so on, using a technique known as soul retrieval. This is based on the belief that when people undergo traumatic events in their lives, pieces of their souls break off to take the trauma away. The neo-shaman uses spiritual healing to return the lost soul pieces and to bring positive energy to the client who can use this power to cure his or her problems.

The drum can be a useful instrument in this type of shamanistic healing. Frank Lawlis, a neo-shaman who works in a clinic in Texas specializing in healing chronic pain, found that patients using modern pain medications often experience deep depression as a side effect. He was

Neo-Shamanistic Healing

Myron Eshowsky practices neo-shamanistic healing techniques. In the following article, posted on the Foundation for Shamanic Studies Web site, Eshowsky describes how he used his shamanic knowledge to heal a troubled surgeon:

The husband of a good friend came to see if I could offer some healing for what had been for him a distressing year. A world-renowned surgeon, he had not been able to practice for a year. His problems began when he passed out during a surgery. The immediate concern was the possibility of a heart attack. He was hospitalized, but no obvious medical problems could be found. Among his symptoms was a loss of feeling in his dominant hand along with the beginnings of a tremor. . . .

Eventually, he was diagnosed as having an anxiety disorder. . . . Anti-anxiety medication . . . [was] prescribed. While he felt less anxious, the symptoms continued.

. . . In my interview with him, I found his description of his process to be more like a man at war with himself. Internally, he was battling with voices of self-judgment and self-sabotage. . . .

With this information, I had the surgeon journey to the spirit of his conflict. He met a voraciously angry monster being. In the journey he received guidance on how to honor this spirit and what it needed. A representation of the spirit was made. . . . He put this figurine in his yard by a large tree. Here a shrine to the spirit was built, daily food offerings left, and a song sung. This ritual was to be observed from the new moon to the next new moon.

Within a couple of days, all symptoms were completely alleviated. The surgeon returned to the operating room shortly thereafter. Three years later, he remains symptom-free and doing what he loves.

able to relieve these symptoms by using the sound of the drum. The neo-shaman describes why this works:

From a physiological standpoint, we know that a constant audio or visual stimuli at certain frequencies will drive brain wave functions towards a harmonic [feeling]. We also know that the majority of shamans use the drumbeat for their rituals and travels to new realities. Therefore, drumming experiences are helpful to our patients who are in need of new vistas of perception.

We have experimented with the use of a shamanic drumming cassette tape, measuring the relaxation response. . . . It is almost taken for granted now that in most patients the regular beat of the drum will facilitate greater [blood] flow . . . and reduced muscular tension. . . . Individuals have also used the drumming tape for control of their headaches and reduction of high blood pressure.[69]

Wondrous Feats

Neo-shamans do not always work in isolation. In some Asian societies, such as Thailand and Korea, neo-shamans put on performances resembling those of Christian faith healers in the United States, healing hundreds of people at once in a large auditorium or temple. A neo-shaman healer known as Wilasinee attracts people from all over Thailand with her healing ceremonies based, according to James McClenon in *Wondrous Healing*, on "trance performance, symbolic gestures, preaching, and wondrous feats."[70] Utilizing showmanship as well as healing skills, Wilasinee achieves a trance state by performing bizarre feats such as putting skewers through her cheeks and grasping red hot coals. As hundreds of people watched in awe, Wilasinee has also cured dozens of sick people, including those claiming to suffer from blindness and paralysis. After observing Wilasinee, McClenon honed a theory as to why neo-shamanism seems to work:

Two well-established processes help explain spiritual healing: the placebo effect and hypnosis. . . . Placebos are actions or substances that are devoid of pharmacological effect, but are given for psychological effect. Placebos require belief, and their effectiveness is based on expectation. A person who believes that a specific activity is curative can gain benefits from engaging in it. Placebos can cause release of endorphin—a natural opiate that reduces pain—in the brain. Hypnosis differs from the placebo effect because it depends on a special trait, hypnotic suggestibility, or hypnotizability . . . a trait that allows certain people to respond more fully to ritual suggestions. Hypnotic treatments can be successful even if the person does not believe in them. The hypnotic reduction of pain does not depend on the release of endorphin, but hypnosis can induce belief and expectation, and, as a result, create placebo effects. Both hypnosis and the placebo effects can induce physiological results: they may reduce blistering after exposure to heat, for example, or reduce bleeding from a wound. . . . [The] hypnotic processes provide a basis for many of the effects associated with shamanic performance and healing. People who are more open to hypnotic suggestion are more likely to be healed.[71]

Instant Expertise

In the years since *The Teachings of Don Juan* was published, neo-shamanists like Wilasinee have gone into business in cities across the globe. Neo-shamans have also published dozens of books and thousands of articles in magazines. Anyone typing "shamanism" into an Internet search engine will find hundreds of Web sites selling admission to shamanistic workshop classes. Products for shamans, such as drums, videos, herbs, and even shampoos and hair conditioners, can be readily found.

Skeptics have criticized the neo-shaman movement not only for its current commercialism but for picking and choosing among a mixture of belief systems. Nonbelievers

A traditional Siberian shaman pours an offering over a fire. Such rituals are the same her ancestors performed thousands of years ago.

say that it is a typical Western rip-off of indigenous beliefs that ignores the difficult tasks, such as fasting and sexual abstinence. As Joan B. Townsend writes:

> It can be argued that such searches for transcendence epitomize the shallowness and superficiality of much of today's supermarket society. . . . Western

society is obsessed with instant expertise and a desire to sample a multitude of things without investing great amounts of time or energy and without becoming really knowledgeable about any of them.[72]

Others impugn the motives of those neo-shamans who consume illegal drugs. Critics say that shamanism is simply an excuse for these people to justify dangerous drug use by alluding to religious or spiritual practices.

Aside from the intentions of the neo-shaman, there is a question as to whether their healing practices really work. In an age of high-tech medical science, the idea of chanting away an angry inner spirit to cure a disease is laughable to some. Critics suggest that those who believe that they have been cured by shamanistic healing were not too sick in the first place and practice nothing more than self-deception.

Regardless of such criticism, legitimate shamans do not recommend that people suffering from cancer or heart disease avoid seeking modern medical help. As Lewis E. Mehl writes about shamanic treatment for a nineteen-year-old patient suffering from terminal lung cancer: "[We] did not begin treatment with the intention of bringing a total cure. Statistically that would be very rare. Although we also begin with the assumption of the possibility of a complete cure, that does not deter us from accepting the reality of death."[73] While Mehl's patient did die, his pain was allegedly eased by the shamanic treatment. And since the patient had no chance of being saved by modern medicine, the neo-shaman performed a seemingly admirable service.

While science cannot explain shamanistic healing, no one can debate that shamans were the world's first doctors. Although their methods have been supplanted by the

Red Hot Burns, Skewers, and Healing

In some cultures, a shamanic performance is part healing ceremony and part stage show. In Thailand, a female shaman named Wilasinee combines shamanic healing with bizarre feats, as James McClenon writes in *Wondrous Healing*:

Wilasinee told me that her treatments were most suitable for "people doctors cannot help." Wilasinee's ceremony included trance performance, symbolic gestures, preaching, and wondrous feats. After she was introduced to the audience, she addressed them briefly, then went into trance. The spirit who spoke through her had a light-hearted attitude yet proclaimed his power to overcome infirmities. Wilasinee extinguished a huge bundle of glowing incense on the palm of her hand, then revealed that her hand was uninjured. The audience gasped in amazement. With the help of assistants, she inserted silver skewers through her cheeks, tongue, arm, and hand. With a huge skewer passing through her tongue, she told jokes, making the audience laugh at her slurred speech and clownish behavior. . . . Wilasinee showed no discomfort, and none of her wounds bled. After the needles were removed, the spirit speaking through her interviewed each supplicant, asking about medical and personal problems. Wilasinee maintained a professional yet concerned demeanor. Sometimes she seemed to know of a person's infirmity without being told. . . . The high point of the performance was the final healing ceremony. Wilasinee went into trance, and the supplicants were brought before her. She placed her foot on a red hot iron plate and then on each person's afflicted body part. Her foot remained unharmed. . . . Some [audience members] described miracles that they had experienced or witnessed. "Last year, I was virtually blind," one woman told me. "After Wilasinee's ceremony, my sight returned completely. Now I come to tell my story and to see the healing of others."

scientific approach, shamanic techniques were in place for tens of thousands of years. With a record dating back to the days of cavemen, shamanism will continue to play an important role among the people of the world who believe in its value.

Notes

Introduction:
The Mystery of Shamanism

1. Quoted in Jeremy Narby and Francis Huxley, *Shamans Through Time: 500 Years on the Path to Knowledge.* New York: Jeremy P. Tharcher/Putnam, 2001, p. 2.
2. Margaret Stutley, *Shamanism: An Introduction.* London: Routlege, 2003, p. 4.

Chapter One:
An Enduring Tradition

3. Joan Halifax, *Shamanic Voices.* New York: E.P. Dutton, 1979, p. 4.
4. Holger Kalweit, *Shamans, Healers, and Medicine Men.* Boston: Shambhala, 1992, p. 9.
5. Quoted in Shirley Nicholson, ed., *Shamanism: An Expanded View of Reality.* Wheaton, IL: Theosophical Publishing House, 1987, p. 5.
6. Quoted in Jean Clottes and David Lewis-Williams, *The Shamans of Prehistory.* New York: Harry N. Abrams, 1996, p. 11.
7. Quoted in Kalweit, *Shamans, Healers, and Medicine Men*, p. 18.
8. Quoted in Joan Halifax, *Shaman: The Wounded Healer.* London: Thames & Hudson, 1997, p. 9.
9. Quoted in Willard Z. Park, *Shamanism*

in Western North America. Evanston, IL: Northwestern University, 1938, p. 23.
10. Quoted in Juha Pentikäiken, ed., *Shamanhood Symbolism and Epic.* Budapest: Akadémiai Kiadó, 2001, p. 79.
11. Mircea Eliade, *Shamanism: Archaic Techniques of Ecstasy.* Princeton, NJ: Princeton University Press, 1964, pp. 148–49.
12. Eliade, *Shamanism: Archaic Techniques of Ecstasy*, p. 168.
13. Stutley, *Shamanism: An Introduction*, p. 9.

Chapter Two: Communicating with the Spirits

14. Eliade, *Shamanism: Archaic Techniques of Ecstasy*, p. 4.
15. Stutley, *Shamanism: An Introduction*, p. 30.
16. Clottes and Lewis-Williams, *The Shamans of Prehistory*, p. 14.
17. Quoted in Narby and Huxley, *Shamans Through Time*, p. 56.
18. Quoted in Park, *Shamanism in Western North America*, p. 28.
19. Kalweit, *Shamans, Healers, and Medicine Men*, p. 110.
20. Kalweit, *Shamans, Healers, and Medicine Men*, p. 112.
21. Quoted in Robert E. Ryan, *The Strong Eye of Shamanism.* Rochester, VT: Inner

Traditions, 1999, p. 124.

22. Tom Cowan, *Shamanism as a Spiritual Practice for Daily Life.* Freedom, CA: Crossing Press, 1999, p. 25.

23. Park, *Shamanism in Western North America*, p. 66.

24. Quoted in Narby and Huxley, *Shamans Through Time*, p. 219.

25. Quoted in Nicholson, *Shamanism: An Expanded View of Reality*, p. 54.

Chapter Three: Healers

26. Eliade, *Shamanism: Archaic Techniques of Ecstasy*, p. 216.

27. Quoted in Eliade, *Shamanism: Archaic Techniques of Ecstasy*, p. 217.

28. Quoted in Eliade, *Shamanism: Archaic Techniques of Ecstasy*, pp. 217–18.

29. Quoted in Lowell John Bean, ed., *California Indian Shamanism.* Menlo Park, CA: Ballena Press, 1992, p. 139.

30. Quoted in Bean, *California Indian Shamanism*, pp. 99–100.

31. Quoted in Bean, *California Indian Shamanism*, p. 139.

32. Bean, *California Indian Shamanism*, p. 94.

33. Quoted in Tom Cowan, *Pocket Guide to Shamanism.* Freedom, CA: Crossing Press, 1997, p. 59.

34. Black Elk and John G. Neihardt, *Black Elk Speaks.* Lincoln: University of Nebraska Press, 1979, p. 197.

35. Black Elk and Neihardt, *Black Elk Speaks*, p. 201.

36. Quoted in John Lee Maddox, *The Medicine Man.* New York: Macmillan, 1925, p. 107.

37. Mark J. Plotkin, *Tales of a Shaman's Apprentice.* New York: Viking, 1993, p. 97.

38. Maddox, *The Medicine Man*, p. 91.

39. Quoted in Maddox, *The Medicine Man*, p. 109.

Chapter Four: Evil Shamans

40. Ekkehart Malotki and Ken Gary, *Hopi Stories of Witchcraft, Shamanism, and Magic.* Lincoln: University of Nebraska Press, 2001, p. xiii.

41. Morris E. Opler, *Apache Odyssey: A Journey Between Two Worlds.* New York: Irvington, 1983, p. 116.

42. William Howells, *The Heathens: Primitive Man and His Religions.* Garden City, NY: Doubleday, 1948, p. 113.

43. Merete Demant Jakobsen, *Shamanism.* New York: Berghahn, p. 32.

44. Howells, *The Heathens*, pp. 117–18.

45. Malotki and Gary, *Hopi Stories of Witchcraft, Shamanism, and Magic*, p. xxiii.

46. Quoted in Bean, *California Indian Shamanism*, p. 102.

47. Alan Kilpatrick, *The Night Has a Naked Soul.* Syracuse, NY: Syracuse University Press, 1997, p. 22.

48. Quoted in Kilpatrick. *The Night Has a Naked Soul*, p. 9.

49. James Mooney, "Myths of the Cherokee," *Nineteenth Annual Report of the Bureau of American Ethnology, pt. 1.* Washington, DC: Bureau of American Ethnology, 1900, p. 401.

50. L. Bryce Boyer, Ruth M. Boyer, and Harry W. Basehart, "Shamanism and Peyote Use Among the Apaches of the

Mescalero Indian Reservation," Erowid, June 7, 2001. www.erowid.org/ plants/peyote/peyote_culture1.shtml.

51. Boyer, Boyer, and Basehart, "Shamanism and Peyote Use Among the Apaches of the Mescalero Indian Reservation."

52. Quoted in Daniel Pinchbeck. *Breaking Open the Head.* New York: Broadway, 2002, pp. 148–49.

53. Kilpatrick, *The Night Has a Naked Soul,* p. 10.

54. Howells, *The Heathens,* p. 127.

Chapter Five:
Shamans in the New Age

55. Narby and Huxley, *Shamans Through Time,* p. 75.

56. Quoted in Gary Doore, ed., *Shaman's Path,* Boston: Shambhala, 1988, p. 74.

57. Charles Carreon, "Carlos Castaneda Biography," *American Buddha.* www.american-buddha.com/carlos.bio.htm.

58. Cecil Adams, "Did Carlos Castaneda Hallucinate That Stuff in the Don Juan Books or Make It Up?," *The Straight Dope,* June 21, 2002. www.straightdope.

com/columns/020621.html.

59. Michael Harner, *The Way of the Shaman,* New York: Harper & Row, 1990, p. xxiii.

60. Harner, *The Way of the Shaman,* p. 3.

61. Harner, *The Way of the Shaman,* p. 4.

62. Harner, *The Way of the Shaman,* p. xi.

63. Quoted in Doore, *Shaman's Path.* pp. 77–78.

64. Quoted in Doore, *Shaman's Path.,* pp. 78–79.

65. Quoted in Doore, *Shaman's Path,* p. 94.

66. Quoted in Doore, *Shaman's Path,* p. 137.

67. Quoted in Doore, *Shaman's Path,* p. 133.

68. Quoted in Foundation for Shamanic Studies, "Articles Related to Shamanism," 2000. www.shamanicstudies.com/articles/index.html.

69. Quoted in Doore, *Shaman's Path,* pp. 142–43.

70. James McClenon, *Wondrous Healing,* Dekalb: Northern Illinois Press, 2002, p. 5.

71. McClenon, *Wondrous Healing,* pp. 7–8.

72. Quoted in Doore, *Shaman's Path,* p. 81.

73. Quoted in Doore, *Shaman's Path,* p. 133.

For Further Reading

Books

Peter Casterton, Catherine Headlam, and Cynthia O'Neill, eds., *Goddesses, Heroes, and Shamans: The Young People's Guide to World Mythology*. New York: Kingfisher, 1994. The legends and folklore concerning spirits and shamans among the diverse peoples of many lands.

Tom Cowan, *Pocket Guide to Shamanism*. Freedom, CA: Crossing Press, 1997. A short how-to book containing the basic practices of shamanism for individuals who want to become shamans in order to help themselves and others.

Jeremy Narby and Francis Huxley, *Shamans Through Time: 500 Years on the Path to Knowledge*. New York: Jeremy P. Thatcher/Putnam, 2001. A comprehensive look at shamanism as described through source quotes of various priests, explorers, anthropologists, psychologists, and other Westerners who observed or joined in the practice.

Peggy Thomas, *Medicines from Nature*. New York: Twenty-First Century Books, 1997. Discusses what people have learned from traditional healers around the world about the medicinal value of natural substances.

Web Sites

Foundation for Shamanic Studies, "Articles Related to Shamanism," 2000. (www.shamanicstudies.com/articles/index. html). A site run by the premier neo-shaman training center with ten articles concerning the use of shamanism in modern culture.

Shamanism: Working with Animal Spirits, (www.geocities.com/~animal-spirits). A Web site that lists hundreds of animals and the spiritual wisdom shamans believe these animals possess.

Internet Source

Charles Carreon, "Carlos Castaneda Biography," *American Buddha*, (www. american-buddha.com/carlos.bio.htm). A well-written biography of the author and anthropologist whose books were responsible for the shamanistic revival of the late 1960s and early 1970s.

Works Consulted

Books

Lowell John Bean, ed., *California Indian Shamanism*. Menlo Park, CA: Ballena Press, 1992. A series of articles written by ethnographers, scholars, and linguists concerning the practices of California shamans before and after European conquest.

Black Elk and John G. Neihardt, *Black Elk Speaks*. Lincoln: University of Nebraska Press, 1979. This is the story of Black Elk, an Oglala shaman born in 1863, as told to Neihardt in 1931.

Carlos Castaneda, *The Teachings of Don Juan*. Berkeley: University of California Press, 1998. First published in 1968, this book details the relationship between the author and a Yaqui Indian shaman as they take psychedelic drugs and pursue the mystical knowledge of the universe in the Sonoran Desert.

Jean Clottes and David Lewis-Williams, *The Shamans of Prehistory*. New York: Harry N. Abrams, 1996. A study of ancient shamanism based on the interpretation of cave paintings made in Western Europe about twenty-five thousand years ago.

Tom Cowan, *Shamanism as a Spiritual Practice for Daily Life*. Freedom, CA: Crossing Press, 1999. A book that explores ways people can draw on the ancient practices and powers of shamanism to improve their lives.

Gary Doore, ed., *Shaman's Path*. Boston: Shambhala, 1988. A series of articles about shamanism and its relation to Eastern religions, the modern world, and healing, written by some of the leading experts on the neo-shamanism movement.

Nevill Drury, *Magic and Witchcraft*. London: Thames & Hudson, 2003. A study of many types of traditionalist magic including shamanism by an author who has undergone shamanic initiation rites.

Mircea Eliade, *Shamanism: Archaic Techniques of Ecstasy*. Princeton, NJ: Princeton University Press, 1964. A scholarly study of the roots of shamanism as practiced by the indigenous peoples in the Siberian regions of North and Central Asia.

Gloria Flaherty, *Shamanism and the Eighteenth Century*. Princeton, NJ:

Princeton University Press, 1992. A study of the early Western encounters with shamanism as told through the words of early explorers who witnessed shamanistic phenomena firsthand.

Jeannette M. Gagan, *Journeying: Where Shamanism and Psychology Meet*. Santa Fe: Rio Chama Publications, 1998. A book by a licensed psychologist and student of shamanism that explores the similarities between psychological and shamanistic healing.

Douchan Gersi, *Faces in the Smoke*. Los Angeles: Jeremy P. Tharcher, 1991. An eyewitness account of the practices of voodoo, shamanism, psychic healing, and other mystical phenomena written by the producer and director of the PBS series *Explore*.

Joan Halifax, *Shaman: The Wounded Healer*. London: Thames & Hudson, 1997. A scholarly work that explores the shaman's role as a doctor and his use of various spirits and mystical shamanic techniques and rites.

————, *Shamanic Voices*. New York: E.P. Dutton, 1979. Thirty-six narratives by self-described shamans from across the globe explaining practices such as vision quests, healing, clairvoyance, and other shamanic deeds.

Michael Harner, *The Way of the Shaman*. New York: Harper & Row, 1990. First published in 1980, this study of shamanic technique and belief, written by an anthropologist and self-described shaman, is considered a pioneering work in the modern shamanic renaissance.

William Howells, *The Heathens: Primitive Man and His Religions*. Garden City, NY: Doubleday, 1948. Descriptions of magic, witchcraft, ghosts, shamans, and other beliefs of indigenous cultures written with the biased Western viewpoint typically seen in earlier decades in which indigenous cultures are viewed as inferior.

Merete Demant Jakobsen, *Shamanism*. New York: Berghahn, 1999. The first half of this book explores the cultural and shamanic practices of the indigenous peoples of Greenland while the second half delves into neo-shamanism, instructing those seeking shamanic spirituality on methods and techniques of shamanism.

Holger Kalweit, *Shamans, Healers, and Medicine Men*. Boston: Shambhala, 1992. A book by a German ethnologist that postulates that ancient shamanism and modern science share many similarities and that the primordial healing methods of shamans can be backed up by science.

Alan Kilpatrick, *The Night Has a Naked Soul*. Syracuse, NY: Syracuse University

Press, 1997. A study of witchcraft and sorcery among the Cherokee people during the last two centuries, based on shamanic texts translated from the Cherokee language by the author.

John Lee Maddox, *The Medicine Man.* New York: Macmillan, 1925. A useful study of shamanism in societies throughout the world, written with the typically chauvinistic attitude common among Westerners in the 1920s.

Ekkehart Malotki and Ken Gary, *Hopi Stories of Witchcraft, Shamanism, and Magic.* Lincoln: University of Nebraska Press, 2001. Traditional Hopi stories showing how the supernatural and magic are believed to be a part of everyday life.

James McClenon, *Wondrous Healing.* Dekalb: Northern Illinois Press, 2002. A study of neo-shamanism premised on the theory that shamanistic healing works in the same way as the human capacity for religious belief, which transcends reality and allows people to put their faith in an unproven power.

James Mooney, "Myths of the Cherokee," *Nineteenth Annual Report of the Bureau of American Ethnology, pt. 1.* Washington, DC: Bureau of American Ethnology 1900. A description of Cherokee witchcraft and other mythologies in the early 1900s.

Shirley Nicholson, ed., *Shamanism: An Expanded View of Reality.* Wheaton, IL: Theosophical Publishing House, 1987. A series of articles by researchers, anthropologists, and shamans on many aspects of shamanism, including altered states of consciousness and shamanic tradition and philosophy.

Morris E. Opler, *Apache Odyssey: A Journey Between Two Worlds.* New York: Irvington, 1983. The biographical narrative of a Mescalero Apache shaman as he dealt with the cultural clash between his traditional beliefs and U.S. government forces on the reservation where he was forced to live.

Willard Z. Park, *Shamanism in Western North America.* Evanston, IL: Northwestern University, 1938. A relatively unbiased look at Native American shamanism for the era it was written, primarily focusing on the Paviotso or Northern Paiute of western Nevada.

Juha Pentikäiken, ed., *Shamanhood Symbolism and Epic.* Budapest: Akadémiai Kiadó, 2001. A collection of articles primarily about the symbolism and worldview of Siberian shamanism by a generation of ethnographers who started their field work during the era when the Soviet Union ruled the region.

Daniel Pinchbeck, *Breaking Open the Head.* New York: Broadway, 2002. A personal exploration by the author into the effects of various psychedelic drugs and their uses in shamanism including a thirty-hour tribal initiation by a master shaman in the Amazon rain forest.

Mark J. Plotkin, *Tales of a Shaman's Apprentice*. New York: Viking, 1993. The stories of an ethnobotanist who recounts his travels and studies with powerful Amazonian shamans as he races against loggers to record new plants and learn their healing properties.

Robert E. Ryan, *The Strong Eye of Shamanism*. Rochester, VT: Inner Traditions, 1999. A look at the commonality of shamanic technique and belief as seen in civilizations both great and small throughout thirty thousand years of human history.

Margaret Stutley, *Shamanism: An Introduction*. London: Routlege, 2003. A study of the earliest magical and religious traditions of shamanic belief and the role shamanism plays even today as the basis of the world's major religions.

Roger N. Walsh, *The Spirit of Shamanism*. Los Angeles: Jeremy P. Tharcher, 1990. A survey of shamanism that attempts to show how the practice foreshadowed contemporary medical and psychological techniques.

Internet Sources

Cecil Adams, "Did Carlos Castaneda Hallucinate That Stuff in the Don Juan Books or Make It Up?" *The Straight Dope*, June 21, 2002. www.straightdope.com/columns/020621.html.

L. Bryce Boyer, Ruth M. Boyer, and Harry W. Basehart, "Shamanism and Peyote Use Among the Apaches of the Mescalero Indian Reservation," Erowid, June 7, 2001. www.erowid.org/plants/peyote/peyote_culture1.shtml.

Index

Aborigines, of Australia, 14, 37–39, 42
activities
  of neo-shamans, 89–92
  of witch shamans, 63–66, 68, 72
Adams, Cecil, 81–82
adornments, 23–25
Africa, 15, 66
alcohol, 30, 31
Amazon, 59, 74–75, 83, 84
American Indians. *See* Native Americans
animal spirits, powers of, 39–42, 71
animal symbols, 25
animism, 16
antelope, 42–43
ants, 41
Apache, 63–64, 72–74
Apache Odyssey: A Journey Between Two Worlds (Opler), 63, 72
Apsaroke, 41
Australia, 20–21
  see also Aborigines, of Australia
ayahuasca vine, 83, 84
Aztec sorcerers, 69–70, 76

Balbungu, Allan, 37–39
Bates, Craig, 52, 54
Bean, Lowell John, 54
bears, 41
beliefs
  about sickness, 47, 49
  in alternate reality, 85–86
  in shamanism, 12–13, 28, 62–63
  in witch shamans, 75–77
Black Elk, 56–58
Black Elk Speaks (Neihardt), 58
body parts, adornment representing, 24–25
Bogoras, Weldemar, 33
Brother Moon, 44–45
Buryat culture, 49–52

caftans, 23–24
California Indian Shamanism (Bates), 52–53, 54
calling, 17–18
Canada, 21
Canyon de Chelly, Arizona, 64
caps, 22–23
Carib, 19, 20
Carreon, Charles, 80–81

Castaneda, Carlos, 80–83
cataleptic trance, 33–34
Cator, Dorothy, 58–59
Cherokee, 71, 75–76
China, 23
Chuckee culture, 33
Clottes, Jean, 31, 38
Colombia, 43
communicating, with spirits, 29–30
Conibo, 83
consciousness, altered states of, 29, 33, 34, 38
  see also trance state
costume, 22–25
Cowan, Tom, 39
Creek, 76
crowns, 23

dolls, 69–70
Dossey, Larry, 88–89
Downington, Nick, 18–19
dreams, 18–19, 37–39
drugs
  hallucinations and, 31
  hallucinogenic, 78–80
  negative effects of, 72–75
  trance state and, 29, 30
  see also alcohol; peyote

drumming, 33, 90–92
drums, 26, 27

eagle feathers, 23
eagles, 41
ecstasy, techniques of,
    30–34
Ecuador, 79
effigy dolls, 69–70
Eliade, Mircea, 23–24, 26,
    30, 47, 49
Eshowsky, Myron, 89–90,
    91
Eskimo, 15

Foundation for Shamanic
    Studies, 85, 91

Ga, 63
Gary, Ken, 62, 66
George, Dewey, 52
Greenland, 65–66, 68
Guinea, 63

Halifax, Joan, 13, 48
hallucinations, 31–32, 38
Harner, Michael, 16, 83–85
harnessing power, 18–20
Haro, Pedro de, 35
headdresses, 22–23
healers, as first people of
    tribe, 13–15
healing rites, 47–49
    calling back soul, 49–51
    dancing, 55

foolishness, 58
    herbs that teach lessons,
        55–57
    of neo-shamans, 87–89,
        92–93, 95
    sweating, sucking, and
        singing, 52–54
    traveling to underworld,
        51–52
Heathens: Primitive Man
    and His Religions, The
    (Howells), 64–65, 66, 77
herbal medicines, 55–60
hereditary rite, 14, 17–18
Holm, Gustav, 68
Hopi, 64–65, 66, 71
Hopi Stories of Witchcraft,
    Shamanism, and Magic
    (Malotki and Gary), 62,
    66
Hoppál, Mihály, 22, 24
Howells, William, 64–65,
    66, 77
Huichol, 10, 35
Huxley, Francis, 19, 43–44,
    78
hypnosis, 93

initiation, 19, 20–22
insertion, of injurious for-
    eign objects, 76
Inuit
    shaman masks of, 36,
        44–45
    strong eye of, 46

iron disks, 23–24, 25

Jaguar Shaman, 59
Jakobsen, Merete Demant,
    65–66, 68
Jivaro, 83

Kalweit, Holger, 13, 36
Ket, 22–23
Khargi (devil), 18
Kilpatrick, Alan, 69–70, 76
Kingsley, M.H., 61
Koskimo, 21
Kumeyaay, 54

Lame Deer, 18
Lawlis, Frank, 90–92
Lewis-Williams, David,
    31–32, 38
liana, 59, 60
living apart, 60–61

Maddox, John Lee, 60–61
Maenads, 30–31
magical abilities, 12
Mahwee, Dick, 34–35
Malotki, Ekkehart, 62, 66
Manchu, 23
Master of Animals, 43–44
Mayan culture, 42
Mazatec, 48
McClenon, James, 92–93,
    96
Medicine Man, The
    (Maddox), 60–61

Mehl, Lewis E., 89, 95
mental illness, 45–46
Métraux, Alfred, 19
Mongolia, 88

names, 15
Narby, Jeremy, 19, 43–44, 78
Native Americans
  Black Elk, 56–58
  eagles and, 41
  effigy magic and, 69
  rattles and drums of, 25–26, 27
  shape shifting and, 71
  suppression of beliefs of, 78
  symbols of sickness of, 53
  vision quest of, 34–37
Neihardt, John G., 58
neo-shamanistic movement
  activities of, 89–92
  Castaneda and, 81
  criticism of, 93–95
  healing and, 87–89, 92–93, 95
  traditionalism compared to, 85–87
Nepal, 15, 27
Niassan, 21
Nicholson, Shirley, 46
Night Has a Naked Soul, The (Kilpatrick), 69–70, 76
Noll, Richard, 45–46
Northern Paiute

antelope and, 42–43
name of shamans of, 15
vision quest, 34–35

Oglala, 56–58
Ojibwa, 22
Opler, Morris, 63, 72
Ostyak, 17, 51
owls, 71

Park, Willard, 35, 43
Paviotso. See Northern Paiute
Payaguaje, Fernando, 74–75
Pentikäken, Juha, 24
Perron, François du, 16
Petrovitch, Avvakum, 9–10
peyote, 72–74, 80
placebo effect, 92–93
Plotkin, Mark, 59
poison doctors, 67–69
power
  from animal spirits, 39–42
  harnessing, 18–20
praying mantis, 41
priests, 16

Rasmussen, Knud, 46
rattles, 25–26
raven mockers, 71, 75–76
Reichel-Dolmatoff, Gerardo, 43–44
religion, 15–17

Sabina, Maria, 48
Samoyed, 17–18, 26
Shamanhood Symbolism and Epic (Pentikäken), 24
Shamanic Voices (Halifax), 13, 48
shamanism, 11, 84
Shamanism (Jakobsen), 65–66, 68
Shamanism: An Expanded View of Reality (Nicholson), 46
Shamanism: An Introduction (Stutley), 11, 14, 28, 30
Shamanism: Archaic Techniques of Ecstasy (Eliade), 23–24, 26, 30, 47, 49
Shamanism as a Spiritual Practice for Daily Life (Cowan), 39–40
Shamanism in Western North America (Park), 35, 43
shamans
  beliefs of, 15
  female, 14
  freewill, 18
  reaction to, 9–11, 16
  role of, 12–13, 15
Shamans, Healers, and Medicine Men (Kalweit), 13, 36
Shamans of Prehistory, The (Clottes and Lewis-Williams), 31–32, 38

Shaman's Path (Townsend), 79–80, 86, 94–95

Shamans Through Time: 500 Years on the Path to Knowledge (Narby and Huxley), 19, 43–44, 78

shape shifting, 71

Shoshone, 26

Siberia
bears in, 41
ecstatic episode in, 20
oppression in, 78
shamanistic offering in, 94

sickness, beliefs about, 47, 49

singing doctors, 54

sky, ascent to, 20–22, 33

snakes/serpents, 42

soul
calling back, 49–51
flight, 33–34
retrieval, 90–91

spider webs, 72

spirit of the night, 35

spirits
animal, powers of, 39–42
communicating with, 29–30
guardian, 45

malevolent, 63–65
in plants, 56

strong eye, 46

Stutley, Margaret, 11, 14, 28, 30

sucking doctors, 52–53

Sumatra, 21

supernatural spirits, 29

Swanton, John, 76

Tales of a Shaman's Apprentice (Plotkin), 59

Teachings of Don Juan, The (Castaneda), 80–83

Teleut, 32, 49

tobacco, 19

Townsend, Joan B., 79–80, 86, 94–95

training/instruction, 20

trance state, 8–9, 11, 38
cataleptic, 33–34
methods for achievement of, 29–30, 92
strong eye and, 46

transformation, 38

transvestitism, 14

tree, shamanic, 24

Tukano, 43

Tungus, 8, 9, 18

tupilak, 65–66, 67

Uganda, 15

underworld, travel to, 51–52

vampires, 71

visionary dreams, 37–39

vision quests, 20, 34–37

voodoo dolls, 69

Way of the Shaman, The (Harner), 83–85

whistles, 26, 53

Wilasinee, 92, 96

Wiradjuri, 20–21

witchcraft, fear of, 62–63

witch shamans
actions of, 63–66, 68, 72
belief in, 75–77

Wondrous Healing (McClenon), 92–93, 96

Yakut, 23–24, 26, 51–52

Yanomami, 59, 74–75

Yaqui sorcerer, 80–83

Yurok, 52

Zulu, 15

Picture Credits

Cover Image: Bill Wassman/Lonely Planet Images

Klaus Aarsleff/Fortean Picture Library, 86

AP/Wide World Photos, 73

Ross Barnett/Lonely Planet Images, 64

© Bettmann/CORBIS, 9, 17

© CORBIS SYGMA, 75

Denver Public Library, 57

© Werner Forman/Art Resource, NY, 36, 40, 44, 53, 67

Fortean Picture Library, 10, 70

Dr. Elmar R. Gruber/Fortean Picture Library, 25, 27

Viktor Korotayev/Reuters/Landov, 94

Guillermo Legaria/EPA/Landov, 79

Library of Congress, 21, 41

Iliya Naymushin/Reuters/Landov, 88

© Nimatallah/Art Resource, NY, 31

© Stapleton Collection/CORBIS, 32

Timothy White, 14, 48, 85

© Alison Wright/CORBIS, 60, 84

About the Author

Stuart A. Kallen is the author of more than 170 nonfiction books for children and young adults. He has written on topics ranging from the theory of relativity to the history of rock and roll. In addition, Mr. Kallen has written award-winning children's videos and television scripts. In his spare time, Stuart A. Kallen is a singer/songwriter/guitarist in San Diego, California.